Church Administration and Ethics:
a workbook for church leaders

Clyde Leon Baker

ISBN 978-1-78792-099-6

Scripture quotations are taken from the Holy Bible, New King James Version [NKJV], the Easy-to-Read Version, [ERV], New Living Translation [NLT], Amplified Bible [AMP], Darby Translation [DBY] and Bible in Basic English [BBE]

Contact the author

leonbaker12@hotmail.co.uk

Book design, layout and production management by Into Print

www.intoprint.net

+44 (0)1604 832149

ACKNOWLEDGEMENTS

Dr. Merle Patricia is and continues to be my darling and supportive wife in all my endeavours for more than fifty years now. Firstly then, I thank her profusely. I would have never finished this book without her assistance. I also thank all our five children and seven grandchildren who in their own peculiar ways helped in the process. One of them, Jumeirah designed the book cover. Two others, Amaris and Mattia helped in the editorial also acknowledge here the inputs from friends, colleagues and fellow ministers. Above all I thank God, our loving Heavenly Father without whose enablement none of this book would have been completed

DEDICATED

To

Our 7 grandchildren, at the time of writing

Masai, Zaria, Mikkel, Atiyah, Jumeirah, Mattia and Amaris

INTRODUCTION

The administration of a church involves managing its day-to-day operations to ensure it functions smoothly and efficiently. It often provides that the activities of the church align with the mission and vision and supports the pastor and leadership team. Hence It is a demanding and challenging role that embraces the administration or management of human resource, facilities, financial resources, events, communication.

The administration of a church also requires ethical behaviour. That is behaviour that is defined by the character of an individual – honest, compassionate, truthful, respectful, caring. Hence not only without the proper tools and resources, but also without ethical standards, the responsibility of administrating the affairs of a church can be difficult.

Accordingly, citing over thirty Biblical references and with over thirty practical exercises, the book *Church Administration and Ethics* is the most helpful and effective tool for the subject. It is indeed a workbook for church leaders.

Starting in Chapter 1, with a working definition of church administration and ethics, the book proceeds in the next seven chapters to detail out in practical ways and from a biblical perspective on how to administrate people, resources, operations, cash, events, services and systems. Chapter 9, the last chapter, is devoted to ethics. Each chapter first sets out what is intended for the reader to achieve. Then with the provision of definitions, references, examples and exercises the chapter helps the reader to achieve that goal.

Clearly then the book is a masterpiece. It is a manifestation of many years of Bishop Clyde Baker's experience in the subject area. In it, he also displays his profound academic and professional training. Above all, by this book, Bishop Clyde Baker shows that with God all things are possible [Philippians 4:13]. That includes even administering a church, ethically and successfully for the glory of God.

I highly recommend this book.

Moriba Baker, Bsc. BA, LLB, MBA, PhD
Academic Dean,
Humber College, Canada

About the author

My husband, Clyde, has many years' experiences both in the practice and teaching of church administration and ethics. These he gained from his long years of engagement as a pastor and Bishop, also from serving at leadership and Board levels in the ministry. His positions as the Secretary/Treasurer of Pentecostal Assemblies of Trinidad and Tobago and the Auditor of that Fellowship also afforded him years of exposure in church administration and ethics.

Saved at the age of 16 years, he has been involved in ministry for more than 60 years. In Trinidad and Tobago, the country of his birth, he fellowshipped and worked with the Pentecostal Assemblies of the West Indies [PAWI]. Accordingly, with PAWI, he served as youth leader, Board member, administrator, pastor, bible school lecturer, and auditor. But he also supported pastors and groups that were not PAWI. These he helped particularly to realise their visions and missions.

During his 14 years services as pastor and bishop in the United Kingdom, Clyde also worked closely with other Pastors, and the community. Hence, he allowed the church where he pastored to be used as a place for the homeless, a training centre, the Healing on the Streets programme, MakeLunch project, the National Prayers and Welcome Network, a school, a rental space for other churches and the place for community services e.g. weddings, birthdays and anniversaries.

Over the past 27 years, he has been participating with Uplift International and did missions in 14 African countries. That mission is however about coming alongside others and helping to uplift them to achieve their God- given potentials. He is the Vice

President of Uplift International, of which the President Apostle Alvin Nicholson is the Founder with his wife, Reverend Lena Nicholson. In 2024, the Global Altar Watch [TGAW] of which Dr. Abu Bako is the Founding President, appointed Clyde to serve as their Managing Director. TGAW is registered and headquartered in Ghana, Africa but has a global outreach.

Clyde obtained his ministry training from the Open Bible Institute in Trinidad and Tobago. He also recently began doctoral studies in Biblical Studies. He is the author of four [4] books, including *Starting and Managing Your Own Business* as well as another entitled *Church Accounting.*

Professionally, he is a qualified accountant, trained in the UK. He also holds a law degree from that country. Additionally, he has obtained a master's degree in business studies from Warwick University, UK and a Diploma in Business Studies from the University of the West Indies, Trinidad and Tobago.

He has worked at senior management levels in central banking, the petroleum industry and the manufacturing sector. In those positions he reported directly to the Heads of the organisations and participated in the strategic decisions and directions of the organisations.

For more than thirty years, he has managed his own business and has provided consultancy and management services. He has also been a lecturer in one of the leading schools in business studies. He also taught accounting and finance at the Extra Mural Department of the University of the West Indies. Currently he teaches Homiletics and New Testament Survey at New Jewels Bible Institute in Accra, Ghana.

Over the years he has also been engaged in the Voluntary Sector, especially in the UK where he has been a Trustee at the Homerton Hospital, a Director of a Foodbank and a Volunteer with Victim Support. In Trinidad and Tobago. He also served as Trustee of the national Board of the Salvation Army and the Inter-school and Intervarsity Christian Fellowships – ISCF.

In the UK, he was the Chair of four trading companies and the advisor of many. Over, the many years, he has travelled widely and internationally, including to Europe, Asia, Africa, Canada, USA and the Caribbean.

God has blessed us with five children and seven grandchildren. Our family is closed and knitted. We know that the Lord who has started a good work in us will bring the same to fruition [Philippians 2:7]

Dr. Merle Baker
BA. MA. LLB. PhD-Education

CONTENTS

Chapter 1

Church Administration Defined

Objective

At the end of this Chapter, participants and readers will obtain a clearer understanding and working knowledge of administration but more importantly of Church Administration.

Approach

Provide an understanding of church administration by

a) Definition

b) Examples

c) Explanation.

And in the context of What is Administration

Definitions

The Bible does not specifically mention the words *administration*, *church administration* or even the word *ethics*. But the Bible provides foundational principles for church administration. With many statements and examples, therefore, the Bible gives spiritual and practical guidelines on how the church must be led, organized, and governed.

Colossians 1:18 clearly states *And He is the Head of the body, the church*. It follows then that all administration must be under the authority of Jesus Christ, but it must be Spirit led as well.

Scriptures such as Acts 6:1-6, 1 Timothy 3:1-13 and Titus 1:5-9 indicate how the church must be organized and governed.

The Bible also shows emphatically that the character of the church leader is fundamental in church administration or in administration generally.

Joseph of the Old Testament did not administrate a "church" but he stands out as an example on how to administer with integrity. His story is told in Genesis 37-50.

Briefly, Joseph was one of the sons of Jacob. He had two symbolic dreams that foretold of his future. In the first, his brothers' sheaves of wheat bowed down to his sheaf and in the second, the sun, moon and stars bowed down to him. Jacob, his father, favored him, giving him among other things a special-colored coat. But his jealous brothers sold into slavery in Egypt where he ultimately became ruler of the land, second only to King Pharaoh

Specifically, Genesis 41: 14-57, and 47:13-26 demonstrate how Joseph administrated Egypt's corn resources during seven years of abundance and in the subsequent seven years of famine how he strategically allocated and distributed the stockpiled resources to the Egyptians and the neighboring regions. He did that in a manner that brought great benefits not only to the Pharoah but to many, including his own family and countrymen.

Notably from Joseph's administrative plan were the following:

- Stockpiling vast amounts of grain during the years of plenty and thereby making preparation for the impending years of famine
- Making the resources of the stockpile available for distribution by sales and gaining in exchange vast sums of money for Pharoah's treasury and when money failed, receiving in exchange for the Pharoah, cattle, land and human resources
- Sustaining administratively, the Egyptian population and neighboring regions throughout the seven years of famine

Indubitably, Joseph was able to manage so successfully and efficiently for reasons that included

He lived a Godly life

- Found favour with God and man [Genesis 39:22 -23, 41:41-42]
- Being a person of integrity, discreet, wise and a man in whom the Spirit of God is [Genesis 41:33, 38]
- He was trusted to do administrative work [Genesis 39:4,6, 23]
- The Lord was with him [Genesis 39:3]
- Defining Church Administration with reference to Administration

An understanding of church administration can also be gleaned with reference to Administration in general. Hence, the Merriam- Webster Dictionary defines Administration in the following ways: :

1. *The performance of executive duties e.g. worked in the administration of a hospital*
2. *The act or process of administering something e.g. the administration of justice, the administration of medication*
3. *the execution of public affairs as distinguished from policymaking*
4. *the body of persons who administer*
5. *the term of office of an administrative officer or body during the Clinton administration*

From *https://en.wiktionary.org/wiki/administration,* the following is also said about administration:

a) The act of administering, government of public affairs; the services rendered, or duties assumed; in conducting affairs, the conducting of any office, or employment

b) A body that administrates; the executive; part of government; the persons that collectively who are entrusted with the execution of laws and superintendence of public affairs; the chief magistrate and his cabinet or council, or the councilor ministry,

c) The act of administering or tendering something to another, dispensation of a medicine, of an oath, of injustice, or the sacrament, or oral administration of insulin.

Hence, Diagram 1 below summarises and captures administration as follows:

Diagram 1

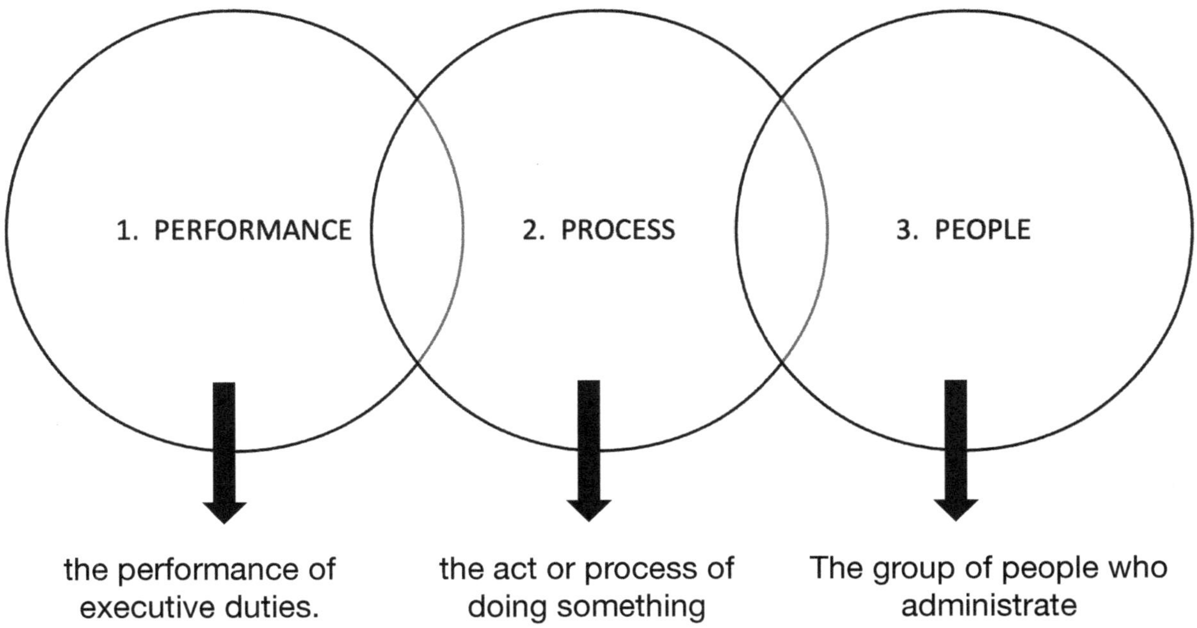

In reference then to Administration, Church Administration then is that administration that relates to administration of the operations of the church. In a similar way there are

1. Public Administration: i.e. **the implementation of government policy and the management of public programs**
2. Business Administration i.e. Managing business operations.

Among the many definitions given for church administration, have come the following:

Church administration is a spiritual service involving the wise stewardship of God's resources to accomplish ministry work. Administration is not an end in itself but a means to serve people effectively while glorifying God .bclr.org [The Bible Church of Little Rock, [located in Little Rock, Arkansas, USA]

This definition focuses on the organized coordination of resources in service to Christ. It is thus like another definition which states:

> *Church administration is the organization and co-ordination of the earthly resources that are available in the service of Christ"*

Hence Church Administration involves managing the day-to-day operations of a church to ensure it runs smoothly and efficiently. It covers areas like staff management, communication, event planning, record-keeping, and maintaining the church's facilities. It often ensures that church activities align with the church's mission and vision, supporting the pastor and leadership team.

In summary then, church administration involves and is not limited to the Administration or management of

People – human resource management

Resources [other] – facilities management

Operations – work management

Cash – financial resources

Events- day-to-day, special

Services – missions and ministries

Systems- procedures

Diagram 2: Administration of

Further understanding

An understanding of church administration can also be gained from the perspective of some leading Pastors. These are all African born pastors. The following have been selected, however.

a) Prophet T.B. Joshua
b) Pastor Chris Oyakhilome
c) Dr. Paul Enenche
d) Bishop David Oyedepo
e) Pastor Enoch A. Adeboye

Prophet T.B. Joshua, died on 05th June 2021 at the age of 57 years. In 1987 he founded The Synagogue, Church of All Nations (SCOAN). The church has a presence across the globe with over 50,000 individuals attending service weekly.

Prophet Joshua emphasized a Christ-centered approach to church administration. His teachings focused on humility, service, and integrity, rather than rigid organizational structures.

Accordingly, his teachings included and were not limited to the following.:

1. That a church should not be run like a secular organization but should be guided by the Holy Spirit.
2. He discouraged an overemphasis on hierarchy and bureaucracy
3. He often criticized churches that focused too much on administration and less on the move of the Holy Spirit.
4. He believed that a well-structured church without God's power would be ineffective.

Pastor Chris Oyakhilome, is Nigerian, born on 07th December 1963. He is an author, televangelist and the founder of Christ Embassy (LoveWorld Incorporated), a Christian ministry based in Lagos. The ministry has expanded internationally, with branches across five continents, including countries such as Canada, Ghana, Nigeria, South Africa, the United States, and the United Kingdom. As of 2019, Christ Embassy reported having 145 branches worldwide. And in 2012 it had a regular membership of over 40,000 in Abuja, Nigeria. These numbers have certainly increased, but current information is not available.

Pastor Chris Oyakhilome teaches extensively on church administration with an approach that is deeply rooted in the Word of God, the Holy Spirit, and a structured yet spiritually dynamic system.

Hence his teachings and beliefs with respect to church administration include the following:

1. Church administration should be structured yet guided by the Holy Spirit.
2. The church is a divine institution and should be run based on God's principles, not worldly business models.
3. Order and discipline are essential in managing church affairs, ensuring efficiency and effectiveness in ministry.

4. Departments and ministries within the church (e.g., prayer teams, outreach units, media, finance) must function effectively to support the work of the Gospel.

Qualified as a medical doctor, Dr. Paul Enenche, was called into ministry by God. He was born on 4th June 1968, in Nigeria, He is the founder and senior pastor of Dunamis International Gospel Centre. The headquarters has a 100,000-seating capacity auditorium.

He teaches extensively on church administration with a strong emphasis on spiritual discipline, integrity, and the power of the Holy Spirit. His teachings align with biblical principles, excellence in ministry, and moral uprightness. :

Hence, he holds that church administration must be structured yet Spirit-led, ensuring order and effectiveness. Key principles include:

1. Divine Order: The church should be organized and structured according to biblical principles to maintain effectiveness in ministry.
2. Excellence in Management: Every department, from finance to music to ushering, should operate with efficiency, discipline, and excellence.
3. The Holy Spirit as the Ultimate Administrator: While systems and structures are important, the church must remain sensitive to divine direction rather than being run like a secular corporation.

Further, he believes that church growth must be spiritually rooted and not just about numbers. Key principles include:

- Soul Winning and Evangelism: A growing church must be focused on winning souls rather than just increasing attendance.
- Manifestation of God's Power: Signs, wonders, and miracles should be evident, confirming the presence of God in the ministry.
- Community Impact and Humanitarian Service: Churches must engage in charity, education, healthcare, and empowerment programs to make a lasting impact.

Bishop David Oyedepo was born on 27th September 1954. He is the founder of the Living Faith Church and Presiding bishop of the Faith Tabernacle also known as the Winners' Chapel International. Located in Nigeria the church is on a 10,500-acre campus that houses among others the 50,000-seat church building.

Bishop David Oyedepo teaches extensively on church administration, emphasizing kingdom principles, excellence, integrity, and the leading of the Holy Spirit. His teachings are deeply rooted in biblical wisdom, discipline, and visionary leadership.

The key insights from his teachings include that church administration must be well-structured and Spirit-led. Hence his teachings emphasize:

- Divine Order & Structure: The church should function with order, discipline, and accountability to ensure smooth operations.

- Efficiency & Productivity: Every church department—ushering, finance, media, protocol—must function with excellence and diligence.
- The Holy Spirit as the Administrator: While having an administrative system is crucial, he emphasizes that the Holy Spirit must be the ultimate guide in all church operations

A Nigerian, born on 02nd March 1942, Pastor Enoch A. Adeboye, is the present General Overseer of Redeemed Christian Church of God (RCCG), With over 9 million members worldwide, including over 5 million in Nigeria alone, a presence in 197 countries and territories, RCCG is a large and rapidly growing church denomination.

Pastor Adeboye believes that church administration must combine divine guidance with practical wisdom. His key teachings include:

a) Order and Structure in Church Management – A well-organized church is more effective in fulfilling its mission. He has built RCCG into a global network with clear administrative structures while maintaining spiritual vibrancy.

b) The Holy Spirit as the Chief Administrator – While organization is important, church decisions should be Spirit-led and not just based on human reasoning.

c) Decentralized Growth Strategy – RCCG operates a house fellowship model and regional administrative structures to ensure grassroots impact an effective church management.

Conclusively then and with respect to church administration, these pastors agree with respect.

a) guided by the Holy Spirit.

b) based on God's principles,

c) Order and discipline

d) strong emphasis on spiritual discipline, integrity, the power of the Holy Spirit.

e) sensitive to divine direction

f) Divine Order & Structure:

g) Order and Structure.

h) The Holy Spirit as the Chief Administrator.

In summary, biblical church administration must be guided by spiritual authority, integrity, order, shared responsibility, and a commitment to serving God and His people. It blends practical wisdom with deep spiritual accountability.

Diagram 3

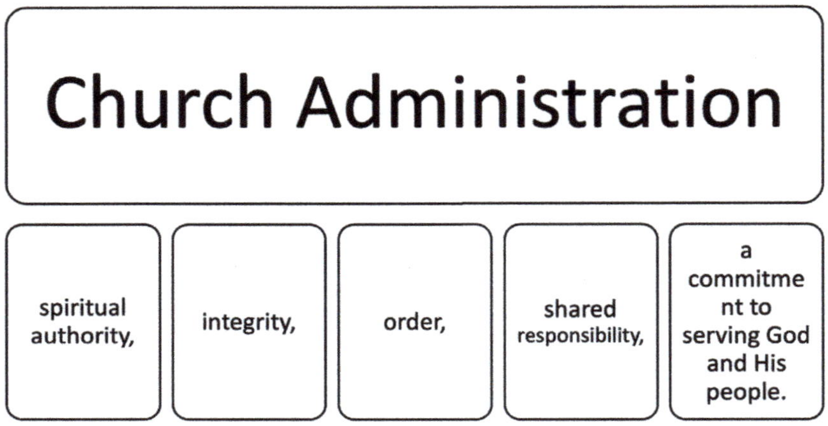

Exercise 1

In less than 100 words give with examples and scriptural references, your understanding of church administration.

Exercise 2

Are the following statements correct

Nos	Statements	Yes	No
1	The bible clearly defines administration, church administration and ethics		
2	Administration is of the world and must not be in the Church		
3	Church administration must be grounded on the Word of God		
4	The Bible is the only source on how to administrate a church		
5	Titus 1:5 is an instruction pertaining to church administration		
6	Ministry of the Word and serving tables are all church administration matters [Acts 6:1-4]		
7	church administration must combine divine guidance with practical wisdom.		
8	All churches apply the principles of church administration		
9	Joseph provides a good example on how to administrate resources [Genesis 41: 14-57, and 47:13-26]		
10	Defining church administration as *the business and organizational processes required to run a church* tell us all that we need to know concerning church administration.		
11	Administration can be taken to mean: Process People Performance		
12	Whereas Public Administration refers to the implementation of government policy and the management of public programs; Church Administration refers to the administration required for the operations of the church		

Exercise 3

Which statement below on church administration relate to the following well known church leaders Prophet T.B. Joshua, Pastor Chris Oyakhilome, Dr. Paul Enenche, Pastor Enoch A. Adeboye and Bishop David Oyedepo

Nos	Statements	Related to
1	a Christ-centered approach to church administration	
2	That a church should not be run like a secular organization but should be guided by the Holy Spirit	
3	an approach that is deeply rooted in the Word of God, the Holy Spirit, and a structured yet spiritually dynamic system	
4	Church administration should be structured yet guided by the Holy Spirit.	
5	church administration must be structured yet Spirit-led, ensuring order and effectiveness.	
6	emphasizing kingdom principles, excellence, integrity, and the leading of the Holy Spirit.	
7	church administration must combine divine guidance with practical wisdom.	

Summary

The Bible does not specifically mention the words *administration, church administration* or even the word *ethics*. But the Bible provides foundational principles for church administration. With many statements and examples, therefore, the Bible gives spiritual and practical guidelines on how the church must be led, organized, and governed.

References include Colossians 1:18, Acts 6:1-6, 1 Timothy 3:1-13 and Titus 1:5-9 .

An understanding of church administration can also be gleaned with reference to Administration in general

For example, The Merriam- Webster Dictionary defines Administration as:

- *The performance of executive duties e.g. worked in the administration of a hospital*
- *The act or process of administering something e.g. the administration of justice, the administration of medication*
- *the execution of public affairs as distinguished from policymaking*
- *the body of people who administer*
- *the term of office of an administrative officer or body during the Clinton administration*

Church Administration then is that administration that relates to administration of the operations of the church..It **involves and is not limited to the** Administration or management of

People – human resource management

Resources [other] – facilities management

Operations – work management

Cash – financial resources

Events- day-to-day, special

Services – missions and ministries

Systems- procedures

Among some of the leading pastors who provide further understanding of church administration include Prophet T.B. Joshua, Pastor Chris Oyakhilome, Dr. Paul Enenche, Bishop David Oyedepo, and Pastor Enoch A. Adeboye

In summary, biblical church administration must be guided by spiritual authority, integrity, order, shared responsibility, and a commitment to serving God and His people. It blends practical wisdom with deep spiritual accountability.

Chapter 2

Administration of People

Objective

At the end of this Chapter, participants and readers will be better equipped to manage the human resources of the church given the vision, structure and required leadership of and for the church.

Approach

a) Explanation – the administration of people
b) Vision, Mission and Church Strategy
c) Business vision vs Biblical vision
d) The Vision for the church
e) Leadership, i.e. styles, skills and competence
f) Church leadership
g) Leadership – Perspectives, Biblical examples

What is the Administration of People

As defined earlier, administration refers to *the performance of executive duties*. In terms of Administration of People, it would mean the duties required for the administration or management of people. That is Human resource management which is defined *as organizing, coordinating, and managing an organization's current employees to carry out an organization's mission, vision, and goals. This includes recruiting, hiring, training, compensating, retaining, and motivating employees.*

Diagram 4

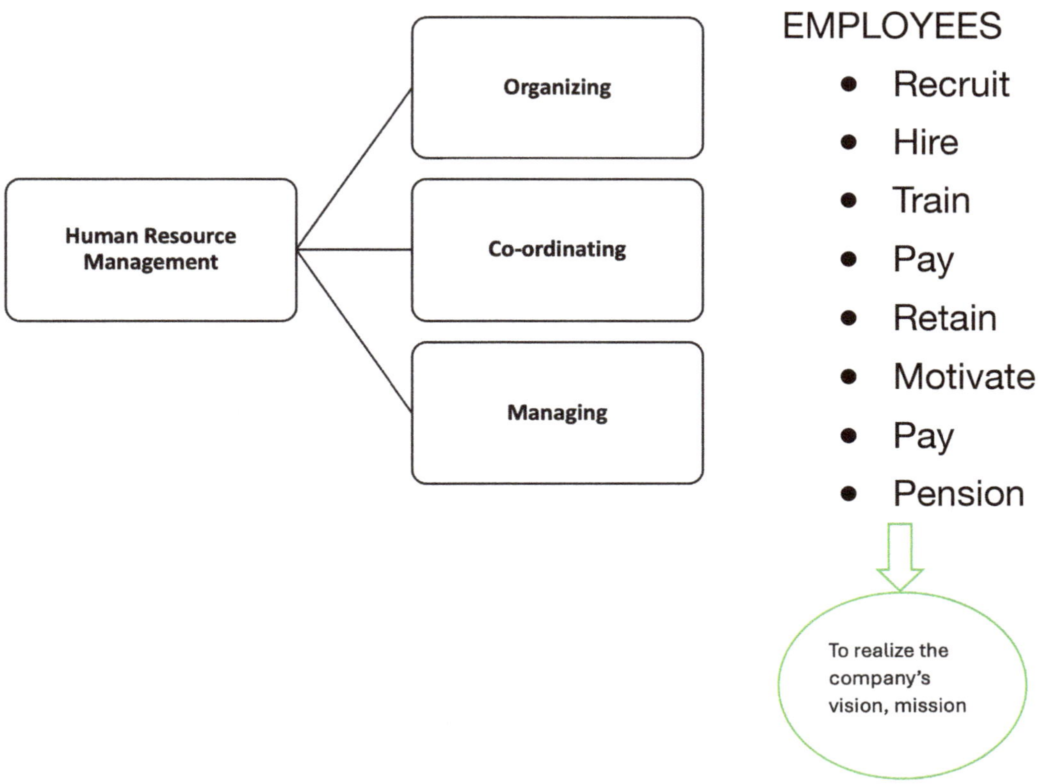

Embedded then in the above is that for effective and efficient administration of the church and in particular the administration of the people or the human resources there must be clearly stated and understood

Diagram 5: Vision, Mission and Church Strategy

The word vision appears in 79 verses in the King James Version of the bible. The word "mission" does not appear in the KJV, however. But the meaning of vision in these texts may not mean the same thing, for example, vision included

a) An encounter with God where He imparted special revelation e.g.
    - Abraham – Genesis 15
    - Samuel – 1 Samuel 3

- Daniel – Daniel 7-12
- Ananias – Acts 9
- Cornelius – Acts 10
- Peter – Acts 10

b) Seeing and revealing of God's plans – Book of Revelation

c) Prophecy – Isaiah and Ezekiel

But a vision in business refers to

a) A company's long-term aspirations and goals.

b) A mental image of the organization's possible and desirable future state.

c) A description of the desired future state of the company.

d) An inspiring statement that shows how success will look and feel

Business schools also teach that Vision must be SMART i.e.

Simple

Measurable

Achievable

Realistic

Time bound

Dr. Abu Bako, the Founding President of Logos Rhema and the Global Altar Watch [TGAW] adds that the Vision must be sustainable.

The following therefore are some examples of Vision and Vision Statements.

COMPANIES	VISION STATEMENTS
BBC:	To be the most creative organization in the world
Google	To provide access to the world's information in one click
Instagram	Capture and share the world's moments
Microsoft	To help people throughout the world realize their full potential
Amazon	Our vision is to be earth's most customer-centric company, where customers can find and discover anything they might want to buy online
South Africa Airlines	Africa's Leading World-Class Airline
Farm Africa	**A resilient, rural Africa where people and the environment thrive**
Econet	Our vision is a digitally connected future that leaves no African behind

Exercise 4

Select three verses from those given below and explain in not more than 10 words your understanding of "vision"

Habakkuk 2:2-3

And the Lord answered me: "Write the ***vision****; make it plain on tablets, so he may run who reads it." For still the* ***vision*** *awaits its appointed time; it hastens to the end—it will not lie. If it seems slow, wait for it; it will surely come; it will not delay.*

Joel 2:28

"And it shall come to pass afterward, that I will pour out my Spirit on all flesh; your sons and your daughters shall prophesy, your old men shall dream dreams, and your young men shall see ***visions****."*

Proverbs 29:18

Where there is no prophetic ***vision****, the people cast off restraint, but blessed is he who keeps the law.*

Acts 18:9

And the Lord said to Paul one night in a ***vision****, "Do not be afraid, but go on speaking and do not be silent*

Jeremiah 23:16

Thus says the Lord of hosts: "Do not listen to the words of the prophets who prophesy to you, filling you with vain hopes. They speak ***visions*** *of their own minds, not from the mouth of the Lord.*

Numbers 12:6

And he said, "Hear my words: If there is a prophet among you, I the Lord make myself known to him in a ***vision****; I speak with him in a dream.*

Daniel 7:13-14

*"I saw in the night **visions**, and behold, with the clouds of heaven there came one like a son of man, and he came to the Ancient of Days and was presented before him. And to him was given dominion and glory and a kingdom, that all peoples, nations, and languages should serve him; his dominion is an everlasting dominion, which shall not pass away, and his kingdom one that shall not be destroyed.*

The Vision for the church

The Vision for the church must certainly be God's revelation and even prophecy, but it must also contain elements from what the business section calls *vision.* Hence Diagram 6 below offers an understanding of this.

Diagram 6

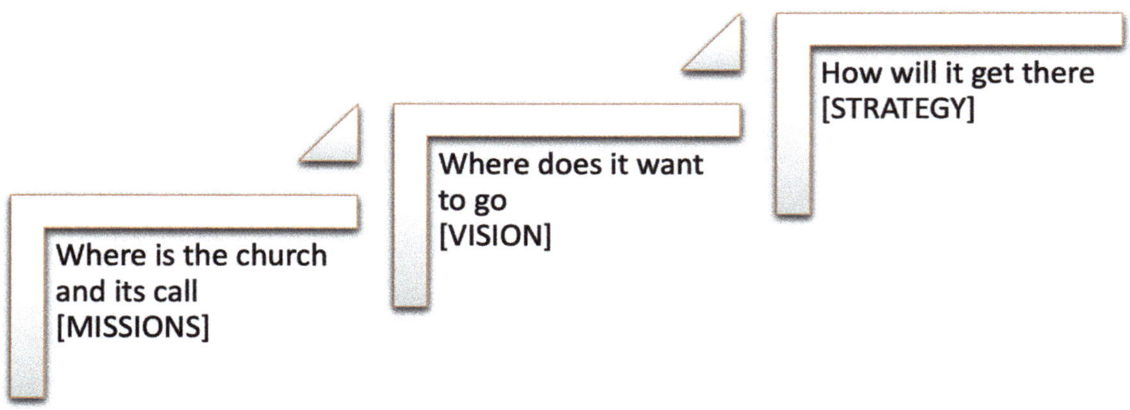

If then the people are to be administrated effectively, then the leaders must not only have a vision, but that vision must be clear and understandable to and by the people.

Exercise 5

You are part of the leadership of the church where you fellowship, in less than thirty [30] words:

- Explain how the Vision of the church was established

  The members were involved in its establishment [ ] Yes [ ] No

  The members were told after it was established [ ] Yes [ ] No

- State the Vision and/or the mission of the church.

Leadership, i.e. styles, skills and competence

What is Leadership? – Church Leadership

Each year, approximately **4.8 billion leadership books** are written. There is thus no shortage of information on leadership as a subject. But to me there are three people who stand out in their contributions to the subject,

Peter Drucker [died 2005]

He was an Austrian American management consultant, educator, and author, whose writings contributed to the philosophical and practical foundations of modern management theory. He invented the concepts known as management by objectives and self-control. He has been described as "the champion of management as a serious discipline". He is one of the best-known and most widely influential thinkers and writers about management theory and practice.

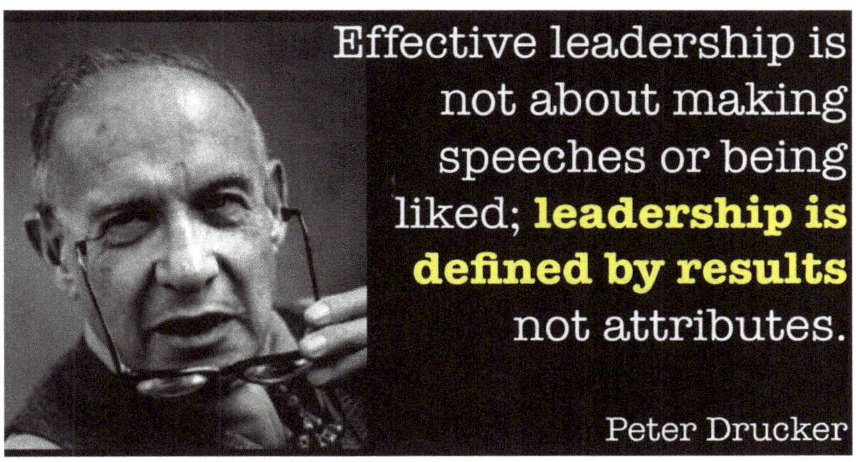

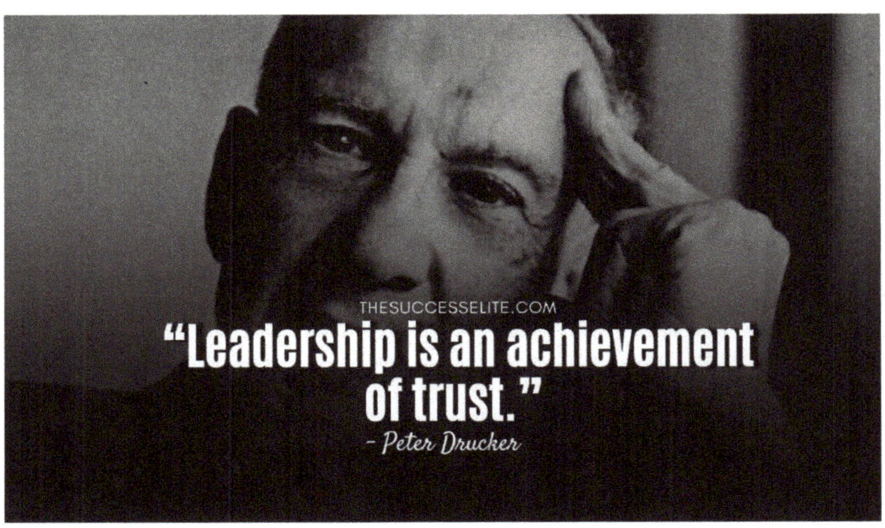

Robert Greenleaf [died in 1990 aged 86]

He was born in Indiana, USA in 1904. The bulk of his career was spent as a management researcher, where he developed a growing suspicion that the power-centered authoritarian leadership style prominent in US institutions was not working. This fed into his Servant Leadership thesis and his book *Servant Leadership [*1977],. He posited that instead of the orthodox leaders being strong-willed chiefs, intent on bending people to their will, servant leaders', those who put the interests and growth of others before their own, were what was needed.

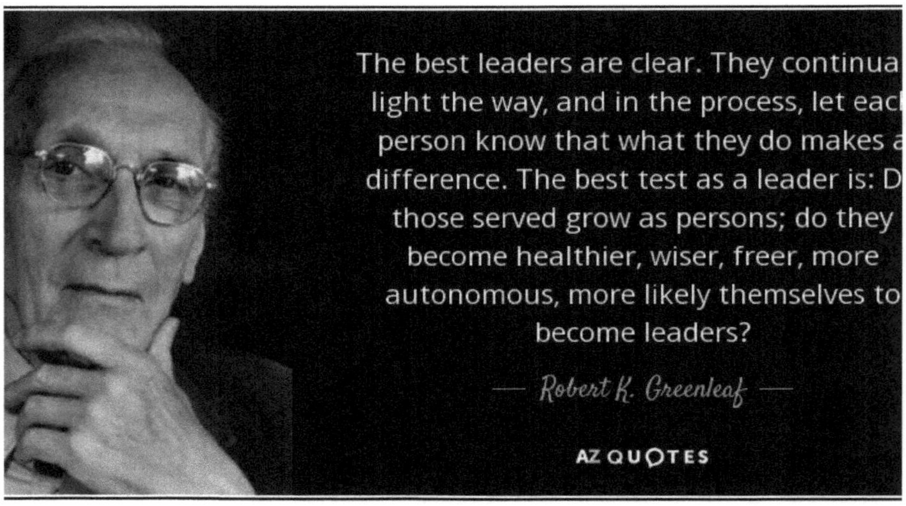

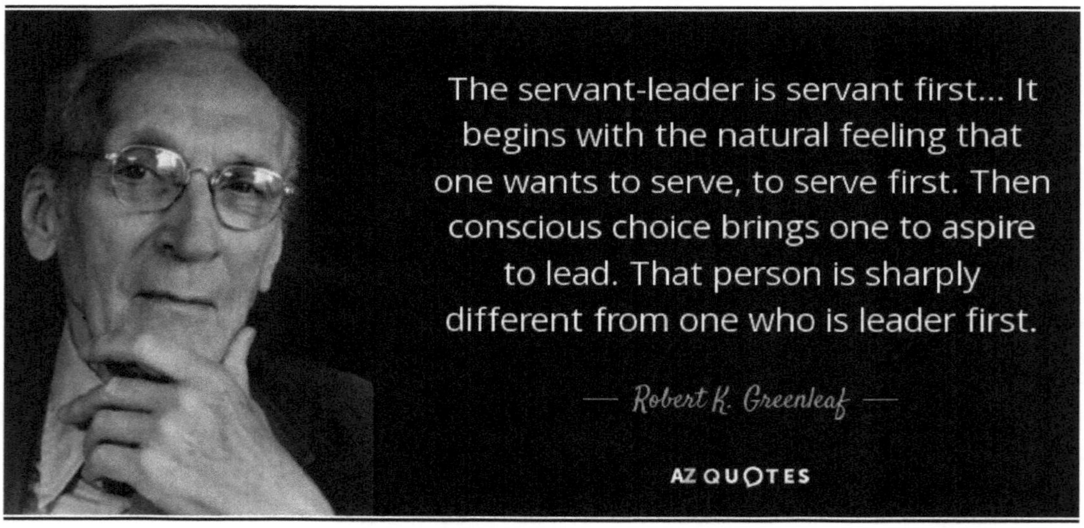

Miles Munroe [died in 2014 aged 60]

He was a Bahamian evangelist and ordained minister, professor, author, speaker and leadership consultant. He founded and led the Bahamas Faith Ministries International (BFMI), and Myles Munroe International (MMI). He was also the chief executive officer and chairman of the board of the International Third World Leaders Association, and president of the International Leadership Training Institute. He was the author and coauthor of about 35 books (with over 16 best sellers to his credit, translated in English, Spanish and Portuguese) and Biblical-related study guides. Two of those books are entitled

1. "The Spirit of Leadership"
2. "Power Of Character In Leadership: How Values, Morals, Ethics, and Principles Affect Leaders"

Exercise 6

Comment on any two Quotations given above.

Leadership – The perspective of leading Pastors

Prophet T.B. Joshua

- church leadership is not about titles but about serving others in humility.
- Leaders should be role models of faith, love, and discipline.
- true leadership is sacrificial, meaning pastors and church workers should be willing to endure hardship for the sake of the Gospel.
- Authoritarian leadership is discouraged instead a shepherd model is promoted where leaders guide their congregation with love and patience.

Pastor Chris Oyakhilome,

Church leaders are not bosses but stewards of God's work. His leadership principles include:

- A leader must have a clear vision for the church, which aligns with God's purpose.
- Training and mentorship are vital for developing new leaders within the church.
- The Word of God must be central in decision-making, administration, and church policies.
- Delegation is key—church leaders should empower others to take responsibility while maintaining unity in the Spirit.
- The Holy Spirit is the ultimate guide—leaders should rely on divine direction rather than human wisdom alone.

Dr. Paul Enenche

True leadership is about service, character, and anointing. Some of his key leadership principles include:

- Servant Leadership: Leadership in the church is not about power but service (Mark 10:42-45).
- Leading by Example: A church leader must be a model of holiness, humility, and discipline.
- Vision and Purpose: Every leader must have a clear vision for ministry and must lead with passion, purpose, and faith.
- Training and Mentorship: He emphasizes raising the next generation of leaders, equipping them through mentorship, discipleship, and the study of God's Word.
- Prayer and Fasting: Church leaders must be prayerful and spiritually alert to withstand challenges and lead effectively.

Bishop Oyedepo

Church leadership is about responsibility, discipline, and servanthood, not about titles or positions. His leadership principles include:

- Visionary Leadership: A church leader must have a clear vision and a sense of divine purpose. "A leader without vision is like a traveler without direction."
- Spiritual Discipline: Every leader must be committed to prayer, fasting, and the Word of God to remain spiritually sharp.
- Raising Leaders, Not Followers: He emphasizes the importance of mentorship and discipleship, training the next generation of church leaders.
- Servant Leadership: A true leader serves with humility and dedication, rather than seeking personal glory.
- Diligence and Hard Work: He teaches that laziness is unacceptable in leadership. "Spirituality is not an excuse for mediocrity."

Pastor Adeboye

Humility and servant leadership are essential qualities of church leaders. His leadership principles include:

- Leadership is Service, Not Power – Leaders should serve with humility rather than seek personal gain (Mark 10:42-45).
- Discipline and Consistency – He emphasizes personal discipline, prayer, and fasting as key to spiritual leadership.
- Mentorship and Succession – A good leader must train others to take over, ensuring continuity in the work of the ministry.
- Faith and Dependence on God – Church leaders must rely on God for direction, not human wisdom alone.
- Raising Leaders at All Levels – He encourages empowering others and spreading leadership responsibility rather than centralizing power.

Exercise 7

Which statement below on church relate to the following well known church leaders Prophet T.B. Joshua, Pastor Chris Oyakhilome, Dr. Paul Enenche, Pastor Enoch A. Adeboye and Bishop David Oyedepo

Nos	Statements	Related to
1	Church leadership is not about titles but about serving others in humility	
2	A leader must have a clear vision for the church, which aligns with God's purpose	
3	A church leader must be a model of holiness, humility, and discipline.	

4	Church leadership is about responsibility, discipline, and servanthood, not about titles or positions.	
5	Leadership is Service, Not Power – Leaders should serve with humility rather than seek personal gain (Mark 10:42-45).	
6	Church leaders must rely on God for direction, not human wisdom alone.	
7	True leadership is sacrificial, meaning pastors and church workers should be willing to endure hardship for the sake of the Gospel.	

Exercise 8

Select any 3 of the above statements and explain how you have applied them to your ministry.

Examples of Leadership from the Bible

Undeniable, the Bible is filled with examples on leadership. That is even on bad or failed leadership. The focus here however is on the leadership that had been demonstrated by the following and the lessons that can be learnt therefrom.:

Diagram 7

Moses -TEXT: EXODUS 18:21-22

21 *Moreover you shall select from all the people able men, such as fear God, men of truth, hating covetousness; and place such over them to be rulers of thousands, rulers of hundreds, rulers of fifties, and rulers of tens.*

22 *And let them judge the people at all times. Then it will be that every great matter they shall bring to you, but every small matter they themselves shall judge. So it will be easier for you, for they will bear the burden with you,*

LESSONS

The Leader

1. LISTENS to wise counsel - ***you shall select***
2. LEARNS from wise counsel- ***place such over***
3. LEAVES work to capable others- ***to be rulers of***

Delegates

Jesus -TEXT: Mathew 20:20-28 [Mark 10:35-45]

20 Then the mother of Zebedee's sons came to Him with her sons, kneeling down and
asking something from Him.

21 And He said to her, "What do you wish?"

She said to Him, "Grant that these two sons of mine may sit, one on Your right hand
and the other on the left, in Your kingdom."

22 But Jesus answered and said, "You do not know what you ask. Are you able to
drink the cup that I am about to drink, [a]and be baptized with the baptism that I am
baptized with?"

They said to Him, "We are able."

23 So He said to them, "You will indeed drink My cup, [b]and be baptized with the
baptism that I am baptized with; but to sit on My right hand and on My left is not Mine
to give, but *it is for those* for whom it is prepared by My Father."

24 And when the ten heard *it,* they were greatly displeased with the two brothers.

25 But Jesus called them to *Himself* and said, "**You know that the rulers of the
Gentiles lord it over them, and those who are great exercise authority over them**.

26 Yet it shall not be so among you; but whoever desires to become great among you,
let him be your servant. 27 And whoever desires to be first among you, **let him be
your slave**—

28 just as the Son of Man did not come to be served, but **to serve**, and to give His life
a ransom for many."

LESSONS

Jesus Christ teaches here that

1. DOMINANT leadership is unacceptable– **lord it over, exercise authority**
2. DIFFERENT leadership – **not so among you –being a servant, and slave**
3. DUPLICATE His leadership - **to serve**

GREATNESS IS SERVING

Jesus -TEXT: JOHN 13:4-17

4 *rose from supper and laid aside His garments, took a towel and girded Himself.*

5 *After that, He poured water into a basin and began to wash the disciples' feet, and to wipe them with the towel with which He was girded.*

6 *Then He came to Simon Peter. And Peter said to Him, "Lord, are You washing my feet?"*

7 *Jesus answered and said to him, "What I am doing you do not understand now, but you will know after this."*

8 *Peter said to Him, "You shall never wash my feet!" Jesus answered him, "If I do not wash you, you have no part with Me."*

9 *Simon Peter said to Him, "Lord, not my feet only, but also my hands and my head!"*

10 *Jesus said to him, "He who is bathed needs only to wash his feet, but is completely clean; and you are clean, but not all of you."*

11 *For He knew who would betray Him; therefore He said, "You are not all clean."*

12 *So when He had washed their feet, taken His garments, and sat down again, He said to them, "Do you [b]know what I have done to you?*

13 *You call Me Teacher and Lord, and you say well, for so I am.*

14 *If I then, your Lord and Teacher, have washed your feet, you also ought* ***to wash one another's feet****.*

15 *For I have* ***given you an example,*** *that you should do as I have done to you.*

16 *Most assuredly, I say to you,* ***a servant is not greater*** *than his master; nor is he who*
is sent greater than he who sent him. ***17*** *If you know these things, blessed are you if*
you do them.

LESSONS

Jesus Christ teaches here that

1. LEADERSHIP is humility - ***to wash one another's feet***
2. LEADERSHIP is exemplary- **given *you an example,***
3. LEADERSHIP is service - ***a servant is not greater***

Servant leaders serve without limits.

Paul -TEXT: 1 Timothy 1:3-7, Titus 1:5-9

1 Timothy 3:1-7

1 *This is a faithful saying: If a man desires the position of a [a]bishop, he desires a good work.*

2 *A bishop then must be blameless, the husband of one wife, temperate, sober-minded, of good behavior, hospitable, able to teach.*

3 *not [b]given to wine, not violent, [c]not greedy for money, but gentle, not quarrelsome, not [d]covetous;*

4 *one who rules his own house well, having his children in submission with all reverence*

5 *(for if a man does not know how to rule his own house, how will he take care of the church of God?);*

6 *not a [e]novice, lest being puffed up with pride he fall into the same condemnation as the devil.*

7 *Moreover he must have a good testimony among those who are outside, lest he fall into reproach and the snare of the devil.*

Titus 1:5-9

** For this reason I left you in Crete, that you should set in order the things that are*
lacking, and appoint elders in every city as I commanded you— **6** *if a man is blameless,*
the husband of one wife, having faithful children not accused of [a]dissipation or
insubordination. **7** *For a [b]bishop must be blameless, as a steward of God, not self-*
willed, not quick-tempered, not given to wine, not violent, not greedy for money, **8** *but*
hospitable, a lover of what is good, sober-minded, just, holy, self-controlled, **9** *holding*
fast the faithful word as he has been taught, that he may be able, by sound doctrine,
both to exhort and convict those who contradict.

LESSON: Leadership is determined by character, Leadership structure, spiritual maturity

Diagram 8

Summary of Lessons from Leadership from the Bible

Moses	Jesus Christ	Apostle Paul
The Leader LISTENS to wise counsel - LEARNS from wise counsel- LEAVES work to capable others Delegates	DOMINANT leadership is unacceptable DIFFERENT leadership DUPLICATE His leadership GREATNESS IS SERVING LEADERSHIP is humility LEADERSHIP is exemplary LEADERSHIP is service Servant leaders serve without limits.	Leadership is determined by character, Spiritual maturity Leadership structure: **Elders/Bishops/ Overseers**: Provide spiritual oversight and governance (Titus 1:5–9; 1 Timothy 3:1–7). **Deacons**: Serve the church in practical matters (Acts 6:1–6; 1 Timothy 3:8–13).

Other lessons of the Bible on Administration of people or the church

a) Stewardship and Accountability

- *"Moreover, it is required of stewards that they be found faithful."* (1 Corinthians 4:2)
- Church administrators are stewards of God's resources—financial, human, and material—and must act with integrity, transparency, and responsibility.

b) Order and Decency

- *"Let all things be done decently and in order."* (1 Corinthians 14:40)
- This supports the use of structured systems and policies that promote clarity, unity, and peace in church operations.

3. Delegation and Teamwork

- Acts 6: Apostles appointed deacons to handle distribution, showing the importance of shared leadership.

d) Financial Integrity

- Paul's careful handling of offerings (2 Corinthians 8:20–21) .

e) Mission-Oriented Planning

- The early church set priorities based on prayer, the Holy Spirit's guidance, and the Great Commission (Acts 13:2–3; Matthew 28:18–20).

Exercise 9

Nos	Questions/Statements	Yes	No
1	A church leader is called and not made		
2	The Bible focuses more on the qualities of the leader, than anything else		
3	Should a leader have on-going training		
4	A good leader uses only one style		
5	Is servant leadership appropriate for the Church Leader?		
6	The leader knows what is best and does not have to listen to others or to take their advice.		
7	The leader hears from God but must also delegate		
8	There is no difference between a world leader and a kingdom leader		
9	A leader is defined by results		
10	A good leader does not seek his/her personal glory		
11	Humility is being subservient to the followers and members		
12	A servant leader is not a servant first		
13	A true leader is not measured by the number of persons that serve you		
14	Jesus favours dominant leadership		

Exercise 10

You are the Pastor of a church in a small community for many years.

Sister Carol has been an active member of the church for more than 5 years. At one stage, she served on the church board. At times, she helps in the counting of the tithes and offerings. She now sends you, a letter of resignation. In the letter she accuses you of mismanaging church funds and says that you have been using the church funds for your own personal use. Sister Carol also circulates the letter to others. She leaves the church abruptly.

Discuss how you would treat with this situation, as the Pastor.

Examples of Leadership from Acts 20:28

In Acts 20:28 [Easy -to-Read Version], Paul advised the elders of Ephesus as follows

> *Be careful about yourselves and for all the people* ***God has given you****. The holy Spirit gave you the work of caring for* ***this flock****. You must be* ***shepherds*** *to the church of God, the people He bought with His own blood*

From this instruction of Paul, the following stand out and are therefore relevant and important in the administration of people

Diagram 9

1. God has given, The holy Spirit gave you, He bought with His own blood

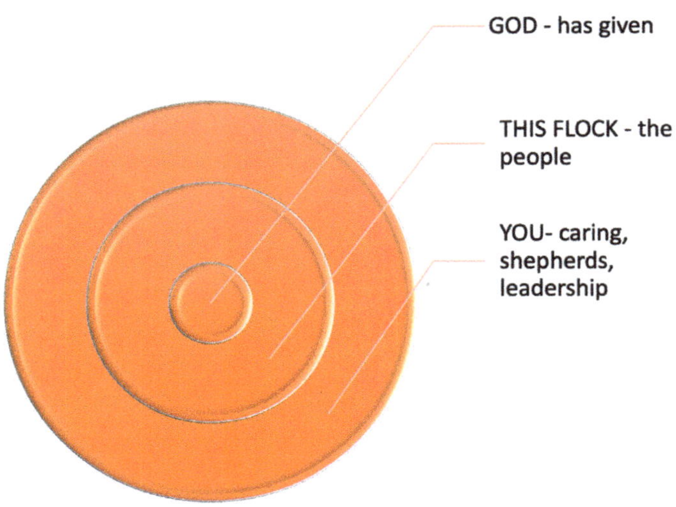

God, the Father, the Holy Spirit and the Lord Jesus Christ are all therefore essential in and for the administration of the people, the flock the church.

In Mathew 16:17-19, Jesus Christ states:

> 17 *Jesus answered and said to him, "Blessed are you, Simon Bar-Jonah, for flesh and blood has not revealed this to you, but My Father who is in heaven.*
>
> 18 *And I also say to you that you are Peter, and on this rock I will build* ***My church****, and the gates of Hades shall not [g]prevail against it.*
>
> 19 *And I will give you the keys of the kingdom of heaven, and whatever you bind on earth [h]will be bound in heaven, and whatever you loose on earth will be loosed in heaven."*

That is to say: He is the Founder and Foundation of the church, the flock- , *the people He bought with His own blood*

And in Colossians 1:18, the Apostle Paul states

> [18] *And He is the head of the body, the church, who is the beginning, the firstborn from the dead, that in all things He may have the preeminence*

That is to say: the Lord Jesus Christ is the authority and has all the pre-eminence. Leadership in the church must therefore reflect this.

Ephesians 4:11-12

> [11] *And He Himself gave some to be apostles, some prophets, some evangelists, and some pastors and teachers,* [12] *for the equipping of the saints for the work of ministry, for the edifying of the body of Christ,*

That is to say: the Holy Spirit equips church leaders with gifts to build up the flock

2. This flock- the people

Exercise 11

Whose people or flock

Are they?

Your People	☐
A people to be beaten up	☐
A people to serve you	☐
A people to minister to	☐
God's people	☐
Sheep/Flock	☐

How do you see the people/members/congregants?

God's people .

Exodus 6:7

[7] *I will take you as My people, and I will be your God. Then you shall know that I am the* Lord *your God who brings you out from under the burdens of the Egyptians.*

Judges 20:2

2 *And the leaders of all the people, all the tribes of Israel, presented themselves in the assembly of the people of God, four hundred thousand foot soldiers who drew the sword.*

Ezekiel 37:21-23

21 *"Then say to them, 'Thus says the Lord God: "Surely I will take the children of Israel*
from among the nations, wherever they have gone, and will gather them from every
side and bring them into their own land; **22** *and I will make them one nation in the*
land, on the mountains of Israel; and one king shall be king over them all; they shall no
longer be two nations, nor shall they ever be divided into two kingdoms again. **23** *They*
shall not defile themselves anymore with their idols, nor with their detestable things,
nor with any of their transgressions; but I will deliver them from all their dwelling places
in which they have sinned, and will cleanse them. Then they shall be My people, and
I will be their God.

Hebrews 4:9

9 *There remains therefore a rest for the people of God.*

2 Corinthians 6:16

16 *And what agreement has the temple of God with idols? For you[a] are the temple of the living God. As God has said:*

"I will dwell in them
And walk among them.
I will be their God,
And they shall be My people."

Revelation 21:3

3 *And I heard a loud voice from heaven saying, "Behold, the tabernacle of God is with men, and He will dwell with them, and they shall be His people. God Himself will be with them and be their God.*

Romans 9:25-26

25 *As He says also in Hosea:*

"I will call them My people, who were not My people,

And her beloved, who was not beloved."

26 *"And it shall come to pass in the place where it was said to them,*

'You are not My people,'

There they shall be called sons of the living God."

Hosea 2:23

23 *Then I will sow her for Myself in the earth,*

And I will have mercy on her who had [a]not obtained mercy;

Then I will say to those who were [b]not My people,

'You are [c]My people!'

And they shall say, 'You are my God!' "

3. YOU- caring, shepherds, leadership

I recently attended a church where it was the new Pastor had to give his first sermon as he was succeeding another pastor who had served for nine years. In his introductory remarks, the new Pastor introduced himself as being a shepherd. He promised that he had come not to lord over the people, but to care for them.

He was correct. The word 'pastor' (Greek *poimēn*) means 'shepherd'. For a shepherd, pastoring involves watching, herding and tending to the sheep. It means being mindful of their needs and fears, whilst doing what is best for them even if they do not understand it. It is much more than just reacting to expressions of desire. Biblical pastoring ultimately seeks to empower people to grow in maturity as a disciple of Christ.

It must then be the understanding in administering the people, the pastor is there to serve. Diagram 10 below says this and more.:

Diagram 10: SERVICE OF THE PASTOR

Leading		Guarding
Shepherding		Supporting
Teaching/Edifying		Ministry of the word
Caring Counselling		Prayer Growth and maturity

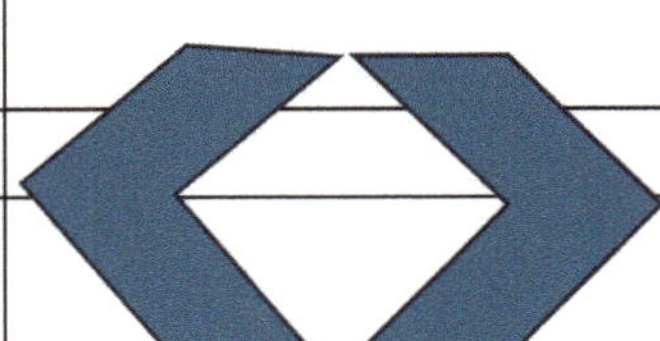

Exercise 12

In your administration of the members of the church explain the three areas that you serve in the most and why

Summary

Administration of People means the duties required for the administration or management of people. That is Human resource management which is defined *as organizing, coordinating, and managing an organization's current employees to carry out an organization's mission, vision, and goals. This includes recruiting, hiring, training, compensating, retaining, and motivating employees*.

For effective and efficient administration of the church and in particular the administration of the people or the human resources there must be clearly stated and understood – Vision, Mission and church strategy and leadership [styles, skills and competence]

Biblical vision included

- An encounter with God where He imparted special revelation e.g.
- Seeing and revealing of God's plans – Book of Revelation
- Prophecy – Isaiah and Ezekiel

But a vision in business refers to

- A company's long-term aspirations and goals.
- A mental image of the organization's possible and desirable future state.
- A description of the desired future state of the company.
- An inspiring statement that shows how success will look and feel

The Vision for the church must certainly be God's revelation and even prophecy, but it must also contain elements from what the business section calls *vision.*

Understanding of Leadership, i.e. styles, skills and competence and in particular Church Leadership were provided from the perspectives of Peter Drucker, Robert Greenleaf, and Miles Munroe as well as from leading Pastors of African descent. More importantly, lessons were taken from the leadership styles and teachings of Moses, the Lord Jesus Christ and the Apostle Paul. The lessons included and were not limited to

- Delegation
- Greatness is in serving
- Servant leaders serve without limits
- Leadership is determined by character, Spiritual maturity

- Stewardship and accountability
- Order and decency
- Delegation and Teamwork
- Financial integrity
- Mission oriented planning

Acts 20:28 [ERV] helps further in understanding the administration of people. That verse states:

> *Be careful about yourselves and for all the people* ***God has given you****. The holy Spirit gave you the work of caring for* ***this flock****. You must be* ***shepherds*** *to the church of God, the people He bought with His own blood*

From this instruction can be learnt the following:

of Paul, the following stand out and are therefore relevant and important in the administration of people

1. God has given the people. The holy Spirit gave you the caring for this flock, He Jesus Christ, bought the people, the flock with His own blood
2. This flock- they are God's people, not yours
3. YOU- the leader, the pastor has then the responsibility of caring, being shepherds and leading.

Diagram 11: SERVICE OF THE PASTOR

Leading		Guarding
Shepherding		Supporting

Teaching/Edifying		Ministry of the word
Caring Counselling		Prayer Growth and maturity

Chapter 3

Administration of Resources [other]

Objective

Human Resources and Cash Resources are not the only resources that have to be administered in the church. There are other Physical resources such as land, building, motor vehicle. This Chapter aims at teaching participants how to administer these other resources

Approach

Inclusion in the Administration of Resources [Other]

1. Acquisition
2. Usage
3. Maintenance
4. Disposal
5. Recording

Administration of Resources [Other]

Table 1

Nos	Scriptures	Comments
	Acts 4:32–35 *"All the believers were one in heart and mind. No one claimed that any of their possessions was their own, but they shared everything they had..."*	This shows the early church's practice of communal ownership and responsible distribution by the apostles. Items brought to the church were treated with sacred trust.
	Acts 5:1–11 [1]*But a certain man named Ananias, with Sapphira his wife, sold a possession.* [2]*And he kept back part of the proceeds, his wife also being aware of it, and brought a certain part and laid it at the apostles' feet.* [3]*But Peter said, "Ananias, why has Satan filled your heart to lie to the Holy Spirit and keep back part of the price of the land for yourself?* [4]*While it remained, was it not your own? And after it was sold, was it not in your own control? Why have you conceived this* thing in your heart? You have not lied to men but to God."	This passage is a warning about dishonesty and misappropriation of goods meant for the church. Ananias and Sapphira lied about their donation, and God judged them severely. It underlines the seriousness of dealing with what is consecrated to God.

Nos	Scriptures	Comments
	Malachi 3:8–10 *"Will a man rob God? Yet you rob me. But you ask, 'How are we robbing you?' In tithes and offerings..."*	This speaks to the misuse or withholding of resources that belong to God's house, showing that items or funds set apart for God's purposes must be handled faithfully.
	1 Corinthians 4:1–2 *"This, then, is how you ought to regard us: as servants of Christ and as those entrusted with the mysteries God has revealed. Now it is required that those who have been given trust must prove faithful."*	While not about physical items per se, this verse establishes a general principle: stewards must be faithful with what they are entrusted with, including property, finances, and other church resources.
	Leviticus 27:30–32 *"A tithe of everything from the land... belongs to the Lord; it is holy to the Lord."*	The tithe, part of which supported the temple (and by extension, what we might call "church operations" today), was to be treated as sacred. This principle of reverence for God's portion still applies.
	1 Chronicles 29:14–17 14 But who *am* I, and who *are* my people, That we should be able to offer so willingly as this? For all things *come* from You, And [a]of Your own we have given You. 15 For we *are* [b]aliens and [c]pilgrims before You, As *were* all our fathers; Our days on earth *are* as a shadow, And without hope. 16 "O Lord our God, all this abundance that we have prepared to build You a house for Your holy name is from Your hand and *is* all Your own. 17 I know also, my God, that You test the heart and have pleasure in uprightness. As for me, in the uprightness of my heart I have willingly offered all these *things;* and now with joy I have seen Your people, who are present here to offer willingly to You	David acknowledges that everything given to God for the temple came from God's own hand. It illustrates the view that all material offerings belong to God and should be treated accordingly.

These verses together highlight themes of:

- Stewardship and honesty (Acts 5; 1 Corinthians 4)
- Sacredness of church offerings and property (Malachi 3; Leviticus 27)
- Communal care and equity (Acts 4)
- Accountability to God for how church resources are used (1 Chronicles 29)

The Administration of Resources [other] include

Diagram 12: Non-Current Assets

The acquisition

The acquisition of non-current assets e.g. land, building, equipment are obtained by purchase or donation/gift. The critical issues in either case are:

- The process
- The recording

There must be documents and a paper trail. For example, if there is the need for the purchase of say 10 chairs for the church, the process should begin with a documented request. That would be followed by the person responsible for making an order with the supplier that presents the best offer. Finally, for payment for the purchase, other documents such as delivery notes, and invoice will arise. Payment may then be by cheque or by cash.

The above process also must be recorded, and the documents filed. The records then will include entries in the cash book to show the payment made. Records will be shown also in a register to provide details of the 10 chairs purchased. Documents such as the purchase request, purchase order [copy], the delivery note, and the invoice will also be filed.

Diagram 13: Acquisition Process

The usage

The guidance here will include that the item acquired is for the use of the church wholly and exclusively. There must then be appropriate procedures and checks and balances in place to ensure this.

It may be, however, that some items [resources] are required for personal use by a member. For example, a member is having a function at his/her home and requires the use of 5 chairs. This, however, must not be just a word-of-mouth transaction. Documents must come into play providing information on the request for the borrowing of the chairs, a statement of liability and for the return of the chairs.

There must also be the appropriate procedures and checks and balances in place to ensure that the physical resource is safeguarded from losses of all kinds. For example, items such as musical instruments must be securely placed in a safe place after use. That may include the instructions being taken away from the church and place in a safe location.

Consideration also should be given to insurance cover. This will be for cover in the event there maybe loses due to theft, damages, "acts of God" – storms, earthquakes, hurricanes.

Finally, there must be safeguards or guard rails to ensure that there is no abuse and/or misuse of the items. For example, it is not uncommon to see after a church services, children wanting to "play" with the church instruments. Adults may even be found dirtying the toilets, the church property, in acts of abuse.

Diagram 14: Usage Manual

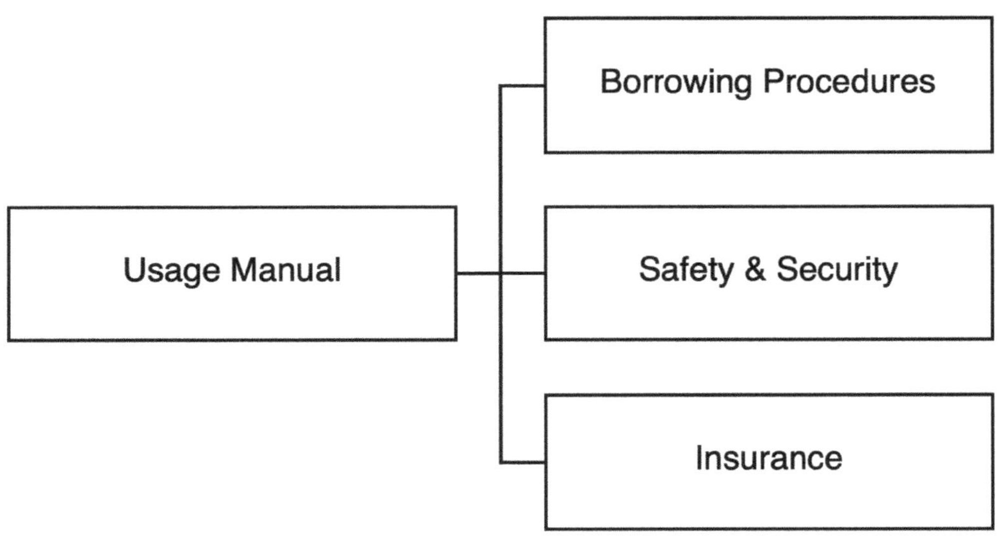

The maintenance

Most churches will engage a person or persons who will be responsible for maintaining the property. Usually, the area of responsibilities will include sweeping and cleaning the inside and outside of the church; cleaning the toilets, cutting and maintaining the church grounds and doing all other things required to have the church and its equipment, machinery and other non-current assets properly maintained. Maintenance then is important for several reasons. Maintenance helps in the following ways:

- Have the machinery, equipment and other non-current assets fit for use
- Extend the service life of machinery, equipment and/or the other non-current assets
- Minimize downtime and costs
- Improve the lifespan of the non-current assets
- Reduce the time, money and any other resource required in the case of disaster.

Diagram 15: Maintenance Activity

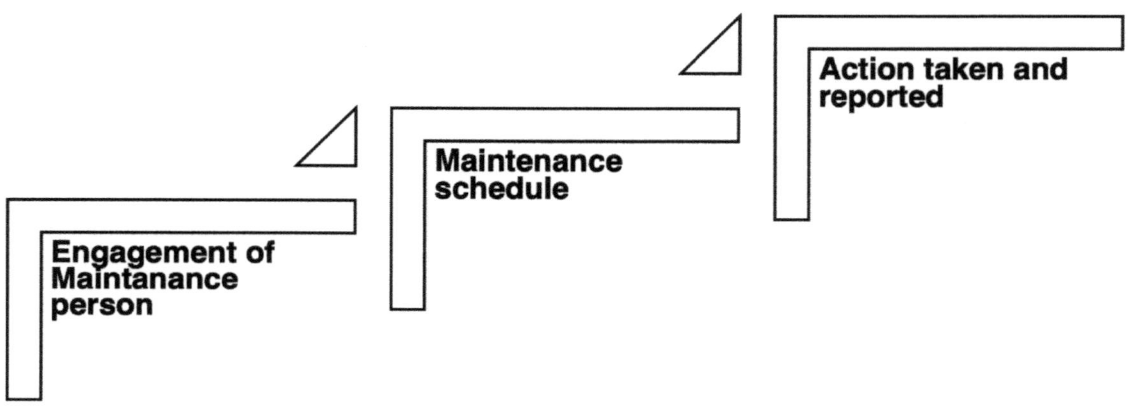

The disposal

In a way disposal is the opposite of the acquisition of non-current assets. It is the process of removing non-current assets that are no longer needed or beneficial. It is also the method of disposing of those assets to recover their remaining value or eliminate them. There must then be physical movement as well as a record made to show that the item has been removed from the books.

Some examples of disposing of an asset are sales, scrapping, or donations. One of the significant considerations in the process will be the value at which the asset is to be disposed of. That is how much the asset is worth at the time of its disposal.

The accountant views that value as the net book value. That is the original cost of the asset less its accumulated depreciation over the period.

Motor Vehicle purchased for	3,000
Less Accumulated depreciation	1,500
Net Book Value	1,500

[NB. Depreciation is the loss in the value of an asset because of use, wear and/or deterioration]

Diagram 16: Disposal Process

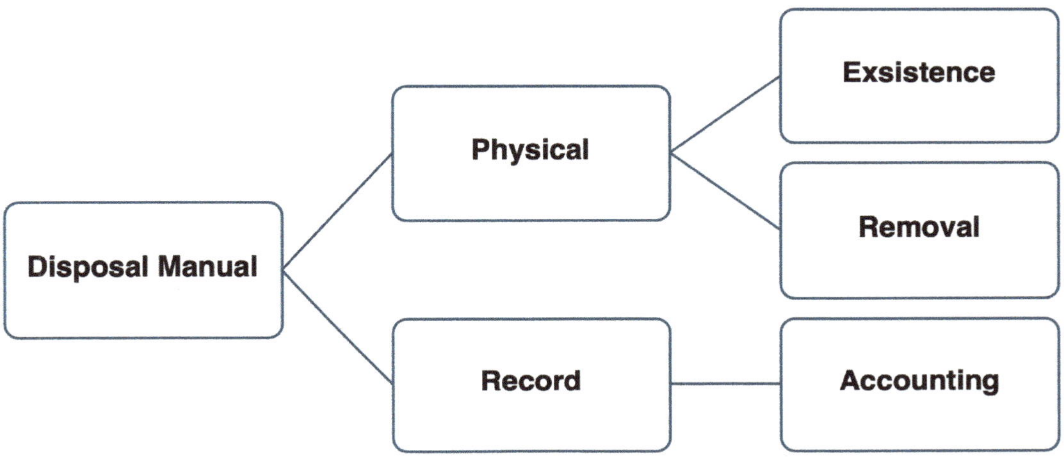

Exercise 13 -Case study

The church seeks to purchase a laptop for office use. Offers have come from the following suppliers:

Supplier A   A brand named laptop for 3,000

Supplier B   Non brand laptop for 2,500

Supplier C   3-year-old brand named laptop for 2,000

At present however the church has only 4,000 out of which 2,000 has to be paid out including a stipend for the Pastor. But by the end of the month, however, there is an expected inflow of funds from tithes and offerings amounting to 2,500

Advise the church therefore on the process to follow in acquiring the laptop most suitable bearing in mind the financial resources of the church among other factors.

Exercise 14 - Case study

Six months after its purchase, the laptop is stolen. The Office worker reported that on her return from lunch she found the laptop was missing. She had left the office door open. There was no one else in the church that day. When questioned the Office worker was unable to provide any documented information on the laptop including:

- when it was purchased
- from whom it was purchased
- at what price it was purchased
- A description of the laptop

Advise the church on what action should be taken.

Summary

The Administration of Resources [other] concerns the administration of non-current assets or fixed assets. The process therefore will include having policies and procedures in place to treat with

The acquisition

The usage

The maintenance

The disposal

The record

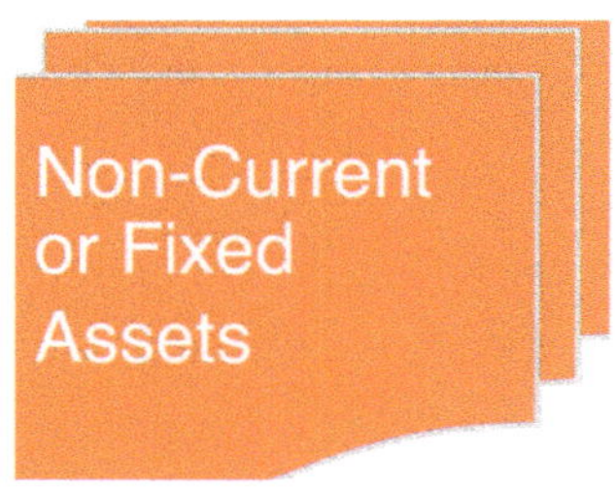

The following scriptures with comments offered useful guidelines on how to deal with items that belong to the church.

- Acts 4:32–35
- Acts 5:1–11
- Malachi 3:8–10
- 1 Corinthians 4:1–2
- Leviticus 27:30–32
- 1 Chronicles 29:14–17

These verses also together highlight themes of:

Stewardship and honesty (Acts 5; 1 Corinthians 4)

Sacredness of church offerings and property (Malachi 3; Leviticus 27)

Communal care and equity (Acts 4)

Accountability to God for how church resources are used (1 Chronicles 29)

Chapter 4

Administration of Operations

Objective

Church operations are a mix of spiritual duties and practical management, all aimed at fulfilling the Great Commission and building up the body of Christ.

This Chapter aims to teach participants how to administer those operations of the church.

Approach

Examinations will be made under the following captions:

- Church operations
- Main functions/operations of the church
- Administration of Main and other operations/functions of the Church
- Structuring
- Managing

Church operations

I was the Procurement Manager of a manufacturing company for eight years. During those years, I worked closely with the Operations department and gained a better working knowledge of what Operations is. It is concerned with administering or managing an entire production system that converts inputs (in the forms of raw materials, labour, overheads, and energy) into outputs (in the form of goods and services for consumers).

The operation of the church is similar in a way. It is the doing of all those organized activities, structures, and processes to make the front-line ministry happen. It includes the smooth running of the back-office functions that are necessary for the church to fulfill its spiritual mission and the practical responsibilities. Factors such as the size or denomination of the church may impact these operations. However, the operations usually revolve around several core functions drawn from biblical principles and church tradition. Hence in most churches, the operations include and are not limited to the following.

Worship and Sacraments

- Worship Services: Regular gatherings for praise, prayer, preaching, and fellowship (Hebrews 10:25).

- Sacraments/Ordinances:
- Baptism (Matthew 28:19)
- Communion/Lord's Supper (1 Corinthians 11:23–26)

Teaching and Discipleship

- Preaching and Bible Teaching: Educating believers in the Word (2 Timothy 4:2).
- Sunday School, Bible Studies, Discipleship Classes: Helping members grow spiritually (Matthew 28:20).
- Catechism or Confirmation Classes (in some traditions).

Evangelism and Outreach

- Personal Evangelism and Missions: Sharing the gospel locally and globally (Acts 1:8).
- Community Outreach: Food banks, clothing drives, health clinics, etc. (James 2:14–17).
- Digital Ministry: Online content, live-streaming, social media presence.

Pastoral Care and Counseling

- Visitation: Caring for the sick, elderly, and homebound (James 5:14).
- Counseling: Spiritual, marital, grief, and life guidance based on Scripture.
- Prayer Ministry: Intercessory prayer and prayer meetings (1 Thessalonians 5:17).

Administration and Governance

- Church Leadership and Governance: Elders, deacons, pastors, church boards (Titus 1:5–9).
- Policy and Decision-Making: Organizational planning and management.
- Church Meetings: Annual business meetings, leadership retreats.

Finance and Stewardship

- Tithes and Offerings: Collecting and managing funds for ministry (Malachi 3:10, 2 Corinthians 9:6–8).
- Budgeting and Financial Reporting: Transparency and accountability.
- Fundraising and Stewardship Campaigns.

Facilities and Logistics

- Property Management: Maintenance of the church building and grounds.
- Scheduling: Organizing events, services, and space usage.
- Safety and Security: Ensuring the physical safety of members and assets.

Fellowship and Community Life

- Small Groups and Fellowship Events: Building relationships among members (Acts 2:42–47).
- Men's, Women's, Youth, and Children's Ministries.
- Support Groups: For recovery, grief, parenting, etc.

Ministry Development and Volunteer Management

- Leadership Training: Equipping members for service (Ephesians 4:11–12).
- Volunteer Coordination: Scheduling and supporting ministry workers.
- Spiritual Gifts Discovery and Deployment (Romans 12:4–8).

Exercise 15

Which of these, however, will you consider to be the main operations or functions or purpose of the church and why. Support your answer with scriptures

Main operations/functions of the Church

Matthew 16

17 Jesus answered and said to him, "Blessed are you, Simon Bar-Jonah, for flesh and blood has not revealed *this* to you, but My Father who is in heaven.

18 And I also say to you that you are Peter, and on this rock **I will build My church**, and the gates of Hades shall not [g]prevail against it.

19 And I will give you the keys of the kingdom of heaven, and whatever you bind on earth [h]will be bound in heaven, and whatever you loose on earth will be loosed in heaven."

Matthew 28:18-20

18 And Jesus came and spoke to them, saying, "All authority has been given to Me in heaven and on earth.

19 Go [a]therefore and **make disciples of all the nations**, baptizing them in the name of the Father and of the Son and of the Holy Spirit,

20 **teaching** them to observe all things that I have commanded you; and lo, I am with you always, *even* to the end of the age." [b]Amen.

Acts 1:8

8 But you shall receive power when the Holy Spirit has come upon you; and you **shall be** [l]**witnesses to Me** in Jerusalem, and in all Judea and Samaria, and to the end of the earth."

Ephesians 4:11-16

11 And He Himself gave some *to be* apostles, some prophets, some evangelists, and
some pastors and teachers,

12 **for the equipping of the saints for the work of ministry, for the** [a]**edifying of the
body of Christ**, 13 till we all come to the unity of the faith and of the knowledge of the
Son of God,

In summary

Taken together these verses clearly remind us that Jesus Christ is the Founder and Foundation of the church, but as such has rightly determined the main functions and/or operations of His church. Diagram 17 below seeks to bring this together.

Diagram 17

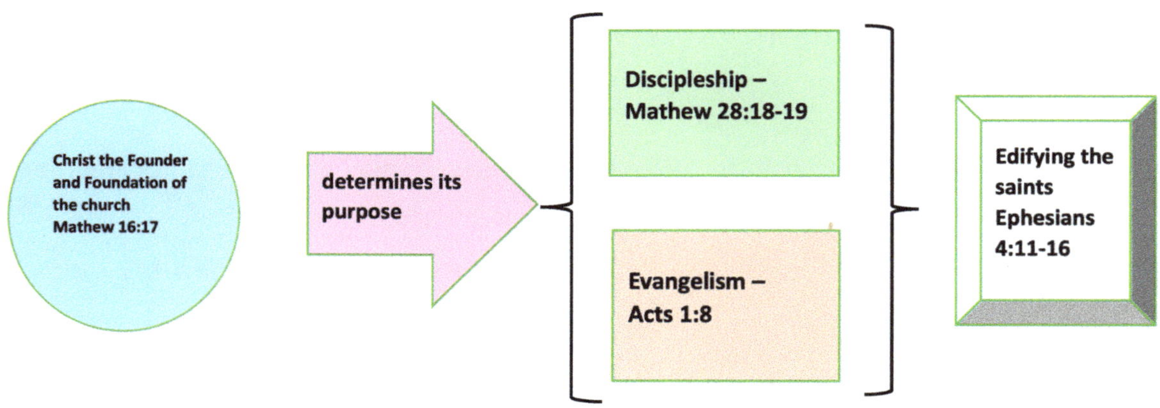

Administration of Main and other operations/functions of the Church

The organizational structure

The organizational structure of a church is the set of hierarchies, reporting lines, roles and relationships that govern how a church functions. Factors such as the size of the church, the denomination, whether the church is "independent" and others can also determine the structure.

Hence, there are many different types of church structures, but the organizational structure of a church typically includes a pastor [leader], a board of directors, committees/departments and a congregation.

The pastor [leader] has authority over the members and staff of the church. He/she oversees the operations of the church. Most importantly, the pastor is responsible for leading and teaching the congregation. The board of directors has an oversight for the finances and the facilities and property of the church. Committees are responsible for carrying out specific tasks within the church, such as planning services, raising money, and managing finances. The congregation consists of members who participate in the services and worship and contribute financially.

Examples of the organizational structures of churches [Source: ChatGPT]

1. Episcopal (Hierarchical) Structure

- Definition: Authority flows from the top down, with bishops overseeing regions.
- Examples:
    - Roman Catholic Church: Pope > Cardinals > Archbishops > Bishops > Priests > Deacons
    - Anglican/Episcopal Churches and Eastern Orthodox Church

2. Presbyterian (Representative) Structure

- Definition: Governed by elected elders, with authority shared among councils.
- Examples:
    - Presbyterian Church (USA)
    - Reformed Churches
- Structure:
    - Session (local elders) > Presbytery (regional) > Synod > General Assembly

3. Congregational (Autonomous) Structure

- Definition: Each local church is independent and self-governing.
- Examples:
    - Baptist Churches
    - United Church of Christ
    - Non-denominational churches
- Structure:
    - Members vote on leadership and major decisions.
    - Pastor(s) lead with consent from congregation.

4. Cell Church or Network Model

- Definition: Church is organized around small groups (cells) that meet regularly and report to central leadership.
- Examples:
    - Yoido Full Gospel Church (South Korea)
    - G12 Vision churches
- Structure:

- Senior Pastor > Zone Leaders > Cell Leaders > Cell Members

5. Hybrid or Mixed Structure

- Definition: Combines elements of different models (e.g., hierarchical leadership with congregational input).
- Examples:
  - Many Pentecostal or Charismatic Churches
  - Assemblies of God (uses a mix of episcopal and congregational features)

Bible Examples

Exodus 18:21-22

Structured with delegation

> 21 *Moreover you shall select from all the people able men, such as fear God, men of truth, hating covetousness; and place such over them to be rulers of thousands, rulers of hundreds, rulers of fifties, and rulers of tens.*
>
> 22 *And let them judge the people at all times. Then it will be that every great matter they shall bring to you, but every small matter they themselves shall judge. So it will be easier for you, for they will bear the burden with you.*

Acts 6:1-6

Structured with separation of responsibilities

> 1 *Now in those days, when the number of the disciples was multiplying, there arose a complaint against the Hebrews by the Hellenists,[a] because their widows were neglected in the daily distribution.*
>
> 2 *Then the twelve summoned the multitude of the disciples and said, "It is not desirable that we should leave the word of God and serve tables.*
>
> 3 *Therefore, brethren, seek out from among you seven men of good reputation, full of the Holy Spirit and wisdom, whom we may appoint over this business.*
>
> 4 *but we will give ourselves continually to prayer and to the ministry of the word."*
>
> 5 *And the saying pleased the whole multitude. And they chose Stephen, a man full of faith and the Holy Spirit, and Philip, Prochorus, Nicanor, Timon, Parmenas, and Nicolas, a proselyte from Antioch,*
>
> 6 *whom they set before the apostles; and when they had prayed, they laid hands on them.*

1 Corinthians 14:33 - Orderly structure

> 33 *For God is not the author of [a]confusion but of peace, as in all the churches of the saints.*

Titus 1:5 - **Establish structure**

> 5 *For this reason I left you in Crete, that you should set in order the things that are lacking, and appoint elders in every city as I commanded you—*

Exercise 16

Draw an organizational structure of the Church where you are in leadership

Exercise 17

Should the Pastor report to the Church Board. Briefly state your reasons why or why not?

The management of church operations

Managing the operations of the church as mentioned above will require of those responsible to

a) Plan
b) Organize
c) Lead
d) Control
e) Make decisions
f) Make effective use of resources
g) Utilize human resources efficiently.

Summary

Church operations are a mix of spiritual duties and practical management, all aimed at fulfilling the Great Commission and building up the body of Christ.

The operations of the church are

Worship and Sacraments

1. Teaching and Discipleship
2. Evangelism and Outreach
3. Pastoral Care and Counseling
4. Administration and Governance

5. Finance and Stewardship
6. Facilities and Logistics
7. Fellowship and Community Life
8. Ministry Development and Volunteer Management
9. Administration of Main and other operations/functions of the Church considers

- The organizational structures
- The management of those structures

According to ChatGPT, examples of the organizational structures of churches include:

1. Episcopal (Hierarchical) Structure
2. Presbyterian (Representative) Structure
3. Congregational (Autonomous) Structure
4. Cell Church or Network Model
5. Hybrid or Mixed Structure

The Bible also provides examples of organized structures of the church.

Chapter 5

Administration of Cash

Objective

The Bible is not a textbook on finance, accounting and money. But the Bible provides some of the best guided and principled statements on the subject.

This Chapter offers the participants a practicable and relevant working knowledge of budgeting, record-keeping and financial reporting. These, however, are from the perspective of a non-profit organisation as the church is

Approach

Examinations will be made under the following captions:

Accounting – Profit vs Nonprofit

The Budget and Budgeting

Record-keeping

Bank Reconciliation

Reporting

Accounting – Profit vs Nonprofit

A large amount of information and literature exists in budgeting, record-keeping and financial reporting for an organisation whose main objective is to make a profit. The church does not operate with a profit-making motive as a trading business. The church receives contributions and donations from its members and others. But these givers do not expect returns from the church in terms of dividends and profits.

Hence, church accounting is the specialized process of managing a church's finances in a way that is transparent, responsible, and aligned with both spiritual and legal obligations. It differs from for-profit accounting in several keyways, primarily because churches are nonprofit, donor-funded entities.

The Budget and Budgeting

The Budget is a cost plan for a specific period e.g. monthly, quarterly or annually. It shows basically

a) What monies are expected to come in e.g. tithes and offerings

b) What monies are expected to go out e.g. salaries, utilities, transport etc

c) The expected balance after taking b) from a)

The Budget is also a road map. It points to where you want to go financially but as with all road maps some adjustments and diversions may have to be made to get you there.

Diagram 18

The Budget then becomes a necessary planning statement. It is thus relevant in all engagements.

Luke 14:28-30 [Easy-to-Read Version]

28 *"If you wanted to build a building, you would first sit down and decide how much it would cost. You must see if you have enough money to finish the job.*

29 *If you don't do that, you might begin the work, but you would not be able to finish. And if you could not finish it, everyone would laugh at you.*

30 *They would say, 'This man began to build, but he was not able to finish.'*

Situations that can give rise to a budget include:

- The decision to engage in a project
- The planning of an event
- The purchase of an item
- A proposal
- Financial planning for a period

The budgeting process

The budget for the church must be carefully and prayerfully developed based on reasonable revenue expectations, and with all expense variances being promptly investigated. The preparation will require as a plan a clarity as to where you want to go or what is required to be done and the required financial resources to get there [Luke 14:28]

Step 1 – Review and analyze historical financial data, say for last 2 – 3 years

This will provide information on sources of incomes e.g. tithes, offerings, donations etc. as well as the changes in these Information with respect to expenses e.g. salaries, utilities, ministry costs, maintenance will also be obtained.

Step 2 – Make estimates of expected incomes and expenses

Firstly, list out the incomes and expenses by types, names or categories and project estimate of what each is likely to be. Table 2 below shows what this will look like

Table 2

	Year 1	Year 2	Year 3	Total	Average
Incomes					
Tithes & Offerings	32,000.00	35,000.00	36,000.00	103,000.00	34,333.33
Special Contributions	1,200.00		600.00	1,800.00	600.00
Building funds	3,000.00	2,500.00	1,000.00	6,500.00	2,166.67
Grants	4,000.00	5,000.00	6,000.00	15,000.00	5,000.00
Donations	4,000.00	5,000.00	6,000.00	15,000.00	5,000.00
Rental Income	6,000.00	6,000.00	6,000.00	18,000.00	6,000.00
Total	50,200.00	53,500.00	55,600.00	159,300.00	53,100.00
Expenses					
Ministry and Program Expenses					
Children's Ministry	700	500	600	1,800.00	600.00
Youth and adult education	300	700	500	1,500.00	500.00
Music and worship	300	400	500	1,200.00	400.00
Missions and outreach	700	800	900	2,400.00	800.00
Total	2,000.00	2,400.00	2,500.00	6,900.00	2,300.00
Administrative Expenses				-	-
Office expenses	1,000.00	900.00	1,200.00	3,100.00	1,033.33
Transport	1,300.00	1,400.00	1,500.00	4,200.00	1,400.00
Insurance	3,000.00	3,000.00	3,000.00	9,000.00	3,000.00
Bank charges	30.00	45.00	75.00	150.00	50.00
Total	5,330.00	5,345.00	5,775.00	16,450.00	5,483.33
Facility Expenses					
Rent or mortgage	4,000.00	4,000.00	4,000.00	12,000.00	4,000.00
Utilities	2,500.00	3,500.00	4,000.00	10,000.00	3,333.33
Repairs & maintenance	1,200.00	1,300.00	1,500.00	4,000.00	1,333.33
Cleaning	1,000.00	1,000.00	1,000.00	3,000.00	1,000.00
Total	8,700.00	9,800.00	10,500.00	29,000.00	9,666.67
4. Personnel Expenses					
Salaries and wages	10,000.00	10,000.00	12,000.00	32,000.00	10,666.67
Benefits (health, retirement, etc.)	1,000.00	1,000.00	1,200.00	3,200.00	1,066.67
Pastor's allowance	5,000.00	5,000.00	5,000.00	15,000.00	5,000.00
Payroll taxes	1,500.00	1,500.00	1,700.00	4,700.00	1,566.67
Total	17,500.00	17,500.00	19,900.00	54,900.00	18,300.00
5. Reserve and Emergency Funds					
Savings for unexpected costs or future projects	3,000.00	3,000.00	3,000.00	9,000.00	3,000.00
6. Capital Projects (if any)					
Renovations	12,000.00		10,000.00	22,000.00	7,333.33
Equipment purchases		5,000.00		5,000.00	1,666.67
Total	12,000.00	5,000.00	10,000.00	27,000.00	9,000.00
Total Expenses	45,530.00	40,045.00	48,675.00	134,250.00	44,750.00
Surplus/(Deficit)	4,670.00	13,455.00	6,925.00	25,050.00	8,350.00

Step 3 – Prepare and Review the Draft Budget

Using Table 2 above therefore, the Average figures of Income and Expenses can be taken to inform the Budget. Provide explanatory notes to the Budget

Diagram 19 THE ABC CHURCH

BUDGET FOR ....

Cash Inflows	**Notes**	**Amounts**	**Total**
Tithes & Offerings		34,333.33	
Special Contributions		600.00	
Building funds		2,167	
Grants		5,000.00	
Donations		5,000.00	
Rental Income		6,000.00	
Total			**53,100.33**
Cash Outflow			
Ministry and Program Expenses			
Children's Ministry		600.00	
Youth and adult education		500.00	
Music and worship		400.00	
Missions and outreach		800.00	
			2,300.00
Administrative Expenses			
Office expenses		1,033.00	
Transport		1,400.00	
Insurance		3,000.00	
Bank charges		50.00	
			5,483.00

Cash Outflow	**Notes**	**Amounts**	**Total**
Facility Expenses			
Rent or mortgage		4,000.00	
Utilities		3,333.00	
Repairs & maintenance		1,334.00	
Cleaning		1,000.00	
			9,667.00
Personnel Expenses			
Salaries and wages		10,667.00	
Benefits (health, retirement, etc.)		1,067.00	
Pastor's allowance		5,000.00	
Payroll taxes		1,566.00	
			18,300.00
Reserve and Emergency Funds			
Savings for unexpected costs or future projects		3,000.00	
			3,000.00
Capital Projects (if any)			
Renovations		7,333.00	
Equipment purchases		1,667.00	
			9,000.00
Total Outflows			**44,750.00**
Balance [Cash Inflows – Cash Outflows]			**8,350.33**

Notes

Use of averages. These should be adjusted to reflect current changes and projections. For example, inflation could cause the expenses to be shown as being higher. Similarly, an expected increase in membership can result in Tithes and Offering being higher.

Step 4 – Approve and Present the Budget

Obtain Budget approval from the Church Board

Present approved Budget to members.

Step 5 – Monitor, Evaluation and Adjustment where needed

Compare actual inflows and outflows to those budgeted and make the adjustments where needed

Diagram 20: Summary - Steps for Budgeting Process

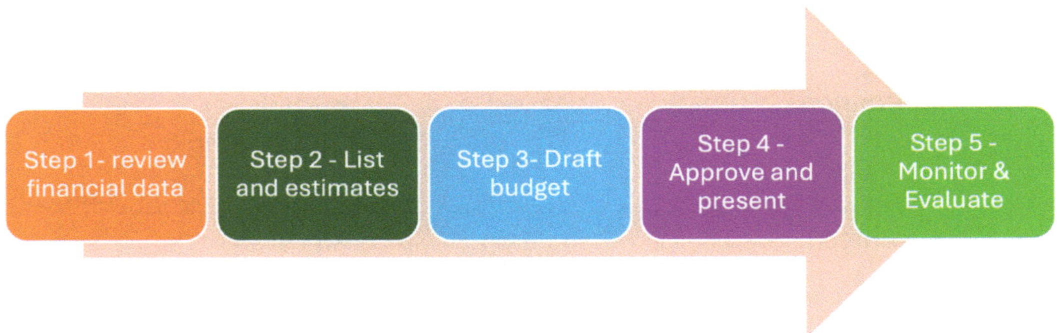

Exercise 18

a) What besides Tithes and Offering are the sources of fund in the church where you are the Pastor, Leader, Administrator

b) In less than 100 words state how you would fund an Anniversary service in the church where you are the Pastor, Leader or Administrator

Record-keeping

The Budget is the planning phase. The actual financial transactions will then have to be recorded, and the results reported. See Diagram 21 below.

Diagram 21

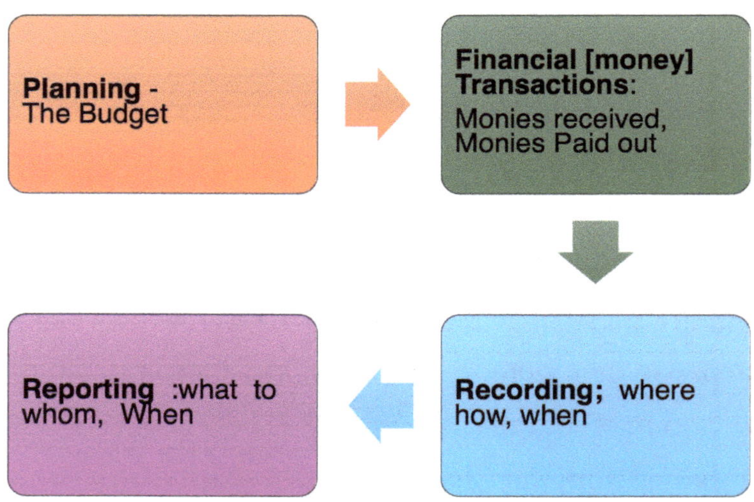

The financial transactions are to be recorded in "books" of accounts. These will include computer systems. The three important points here then are

- How are these records to be made
- Where are these records to be made
- The Format of the records

Wikipedia explains a financial transaction as follows:

> *A financial transaction is an agreement, or communication, between a buyer and seller to exchange goods, services, or assets for payment. Any transaction involves a change in the status of the finances of two or more businesses or individuals. A financial transaction always involves one or more financial asset, most commonly money or another valuable item such as gold or silver.*
>
> *There are many types of financial transactions. The most common type, purchases, occurs when a good, service, or other commodity is sold to a consumer in exchange for money. Most purchases are made with cash payments, including physical currency, debit cards, or cheques.] The other main form of payment is credit, which gives immediate access to funds in exchange for repayment at a later date*

Simply stated financial transactions are those that have to do with the exchange of money for goods and services.

Diagram 22: Exchange of money for goods

Hence financial transactions are to be recorded systematically and in accordance with generally accepted accounting standards. Rules and/or principles are to be followed in the recording of the financial transactions. These include and are not limited to the following:

- In every financial transaction there are two accounts
- One of those accounts is to be debited
- The other account is to be credited
- The debit account is the receiving account
- The credit account is the giving account

"Books" of account

The trading or profit-making company will use different "books" or computer systems to record their financial transactions. These in the main will include

Diagram 23

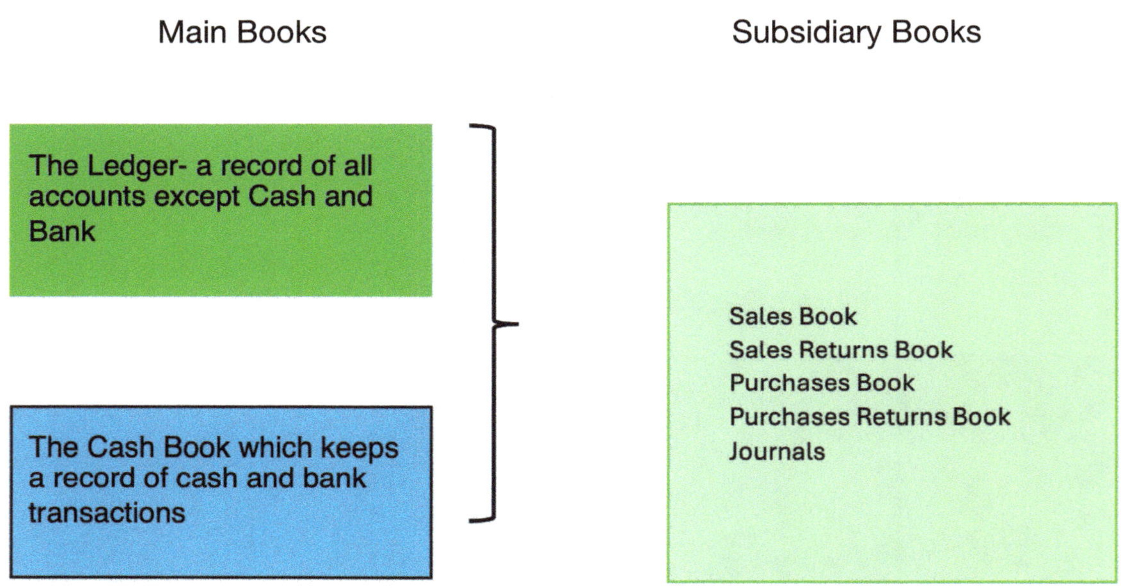

For the church however the main "book" for the record of the financial transactions will be the Cash Book. Diagram 24 below provides an example of the format.

Diagram 24: CASH BOOK

Date	Receipts	Ref	Total	Cash	Bank	Tithes & Offerings	Special Contributions	Building Funds	Grants	Donations	Rental Income

CASH BOOK

						Administrative				Ministry			
Date	**Payments**	**Ref**	**Total**	**Cash**	**Bank**	Office expenses	Transport	Insurance	Bank charges	Children's	Youth	Music and worship	Missions and outreach

CASH BOOK

								Facility Expenses				Personnel	
Date	**Payments**	**Ref**	**Total**	**Cash**	**Bank**	Rent	Utilities	Repairs & maintenance	Cleaning	Salaries and wages	Pastor's allowance	Payroll taxes	Benefits (health, retirement, etc.)

CASH BOOK

						Projects	Reserve and Emergency Funds		Capital
Date	**Payments**	**Ref**	**Total**	**Cash**	**Bank**	Savings	Investments	Renovations	Equipment Purchases

Explanatory Notes

a) This is a Columnised Format of a Cash book.
b) Most stationary stores sell such type of columnized book.
c) Alternatively, an Excel Spread Sheet can be used
d) All transactions must be recorded within 24 hours of their occurrence and be supported by a document. E.g. Tithes and Offering collection sheet
e) The date column records the date when the transaction occurred and not the date the entry was made
f) As much information describing the transaction must be given in the Receipt Column and in the Payment Column
g) The Ref. column identifies the document used to make the record or entry. Document used can include the Cheque number or Invoice number
h) The total refers to the total received or paid out on the day of the transaction
i) The Cash and Bank columns indicate whether the amount was in or by Cash or Bank
j) The other columns show the account

Totaling and Balance

At the end of the month all the Columns of Receipts e.g. Tithes and Offerings etc. and all the payment columns e.g. administrative expenses must be added.

On the Receipt side the Cash Column and the Bank Column must also be added up

The totals of the Cash and Bank Columns on the payment side will be found to be less than those on the Receipt side

The difference to make the Total Column Receipt Cash and Bank and the Total Column Payments Cash and Bank equal must be entered in as Balance.

See Example below

Record the following transactions in the cash book and balance the cash book

Date	Transactions
[01st day] Sunday 13th October	Tithes and offerings Cash 2,000, Bank 1,500
[02nd day] Monday 14th October	Pay in cash office expenses 600
[02nd day] Monday 14th October	Offering Cash 200
[03rd day] Tuesday 15th October	Pay with cheque Repairs 400
[04th day] Wednesday 16th October	Pay with cheque Transport 500
[05th day] Thursday 17th October	Pay in cash office expenses 600
[06th day] Friday 18th October	Pay with cheque Repairs 400
[07th day] Saturday 19th October	Pay in cash Transport 300

Diagram 25

CASH BOOK

Date	Receipts	Ref	Total	Cash	Bank	Tithes	Offerings
13/10	Tithes and offering		3,500	2,000	1,500	2,000	1,500
14/10	Tithes		200	200		200	
	Total		**3,700**	**2,200**	**1,500**	**2,200**	**1,500**

CASH BOOK

Date	Payments	Ref	Total	Cash	Bank	Office	Repairs	Transport
						Expenses	**Maintenance**	
14/10	Supplier A		600	600		600		
15/10	Supplier B		400		400		400	
16/10	Supplier C		500		500			500
17/10	Supplier A		600	600		600		
18/10	Supplier B		400		400		400	
19/10	Supplier C		300	300				300
	Balance		**900**	**700**	**200**			
	Total		**3,700**	**2,200**	**1,500**	**1,200**	**800**	**800**

Bank account

The church should have a bank account.

The following then must obtain for the said bank account

a) There must be at least three signatories

b) Any two can sign at one time

c) The pastor should be one of the signatories

d) Cheque payment vouchers [see Diagram 26 below] must be prepared and approved before cheque is signed

e) No unused or blank cheques must be signed

f) Cheque books and deposit books must be kept in a secure place

Diagram 26

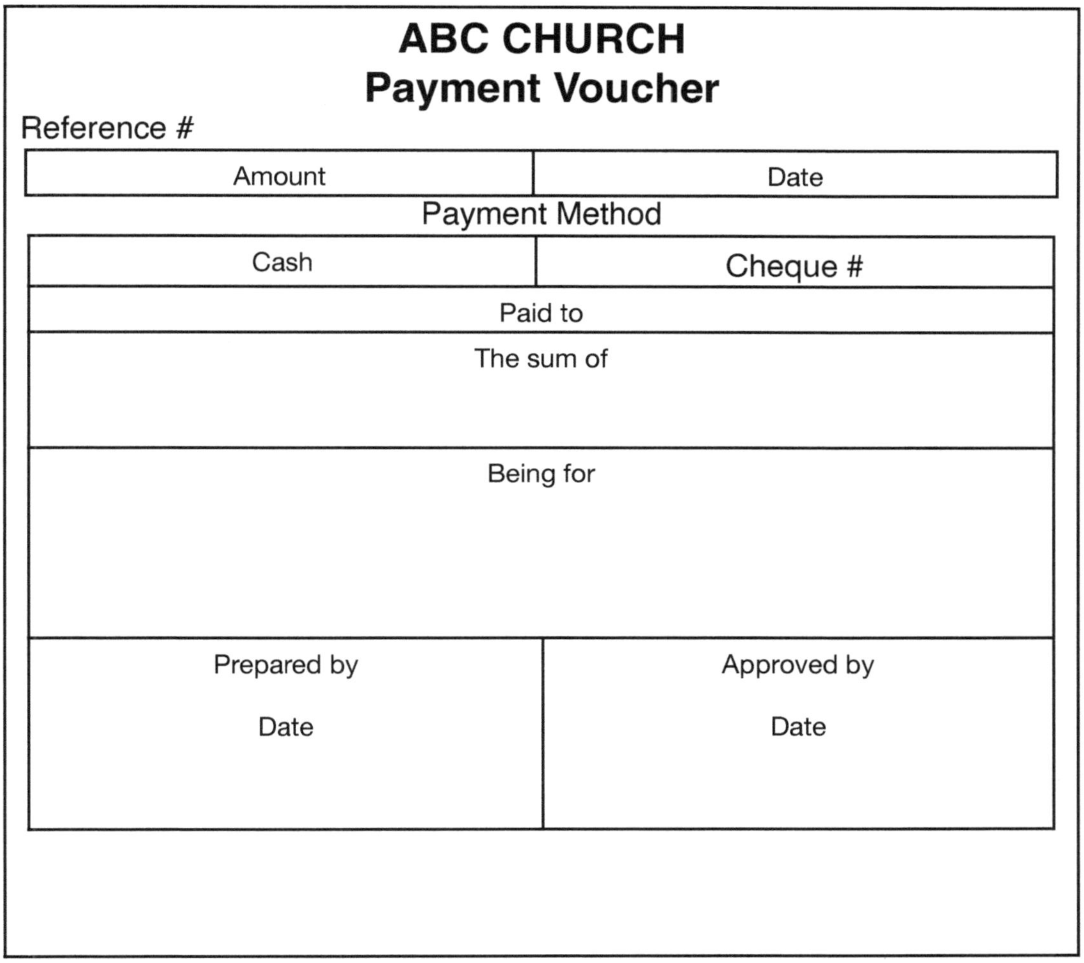

ABC CHURCH
Payment Voucher

Reference #

Amount	Date

Payment Method

Cash	Cheque #

Paid to

The sum of

Being for

Prepared by Date	Approved by Date

Bank Reconciliation

On a monthly basis or on an agreed date, the bank will provide bank statements on the account held in the bank. The balance on that statement will not agree with the bank balance as shown in the cash book.

The reasons for the disagreement will include but not limited to

- Undeposited cheque
- Uncredited cheques
- Payments such as bank charges made in the bank but not in the cash book
- Errors

The Bank Reconciliation Statement therefore is a statement that seeks to reconcile and/or explain the balance as per cash book and the balance as per bank statement

Example

Diagram 27

DEF Bank

Account Number xxxxxxxxxxx

Bank Statement for month ending October

Date	Particulars	Debit	Credit	Balance
15/10/	Deposit		1,500	1,500
16/10	Cheque # 1	400		1,100
17/10	Cheque # 2	500		600
17/10	Bank charges	50		550

In Diagram 25 above, the Bank Balance in the Cash book was shown as 200 whereas in Diagram 27 above Bank Balance as per bank statement was shown as 550.

These then are the balances that are to be reconciled. Diagram 28 below shows how this is to be done.

Diagram 28

ABC CHURCH

Bank Reconciliation Statement

As Of 18th October

Balance as per Bank Statement	**550**
Less Undeposited Cheques Cheque # 3	400
	150
Add Uncredited cheques	0
Unadjusted Balance as per Cash Book	150
Add unrecorded Bank charge	50
Balance as per Cash Book	**200**

Reporting

A financial statement is a document that shows the financial activities of a business. It is the financial record of all transactions the business has made during a set accounting period. For the business the financial statement is presented as

1. Balance Sheet or Statement of Financial position

That is a snapshot of what the business owned [assets] what the business is owing [liabilities] and the net worth of the business [shareholder's equity] as at a particular point in time.

2. Income Statement

This shows total revenue, total expenses and net income. [difference between the total revenue and the total expenses and taxes]

3. Cash Flow Statement

Cash flow is the movement of incoming and outgoing money from the business accounts

For a business, financial statements are important for many reasons. These include the effective management of cash resources, for taxes purposes.

Financial statements – Nonprofit organisations and the church

As a Nonprofit entity, the church must account for its financial affairs to members, donors, grants and to the government for purposes of statutory requirements.

Regulations then require that whereas the content of the information provided by a nonprofit entity as the church maybe the same as that for business the format and name of the statement will be different

Diagram 29

Comparative Financial Statements

For profit business	Non-profit e.g. the church
Balance Sheet	Statement of Financial Position
Income Statement	Statement of Activities
Cash Flow Statement	Cash Flow Statement

Examples

Below are examples of the statements of MOBAK Foundation, a non-profit organisation. That is in terms of

- Statement of Financial Position
- Statement of Activities
- Cash Flow

But such statements, however, for the church will be more in situations where primarily in the case where submissions are for statutory purposes [annual returns], to donors, for grants, at an Annual General meeting and for audit.

However, for the church, a basic set of accounts which can be used for easier understanding, especially in Board meetings and other meetings will be

a) The Receipt and Payment Account

This will show all the monies received and all the monies actually paid out as on a particular date. Using the figures in the example above this then will look like the following

Diagram 30

ABC CHURCH

Receipt and Payments Account as of 20th October ....

Receipts	**Amounts**	**Total**
Tithes	2,200	
Offerings	1,500	
		3,700
Payments		
Office Expenses	1,200	
Repairs and Maintenance	800	
Transport	800	
		2,800
Balance		**900**

b) Income and Expenditure account

This account differs from the Receipt and Payments account in the following three ways

1. The figures or amounts represent monies which have been not only received or paid but those that are receivable and payable.
2. It is the results over a period and not at a particular point in time
3. The difference between the Income and Expenditure is surplus if the income is more or deficit if the income is less than the expenditure.
4. Example

Consider that at the end of the period ending 20th October, that the following was the case

- A brother had paid 300 tithes in advance
- 100 was owing on repairs and maintenance

Accordingly, the Income and Expenditure account will look like the following:

Diagram 31

ABC CHURCH

Income and Expenditure Account for Period ending 20th October ....

Income	Amounts	Total
Tithes	2,500	
Offerings	1,500	
		4,000
Payments		
Office Expenses	1,200	
Repairs and Maintenance	900	
Transport	800	
		2,900
Surplus		1,100

MOBAK FOUNDATION
STATEMENT OF FINANCIAL POISTION
AS AT 31ST DECEMBER, 2021

	NOTES	2021	2020
ASSETS			
NON-CURRENT ASSETS			
Fixed Assets	3	155,960	199,851
CURRENT ASSETS			
Cash at Bank and at Bank		6,812	5,000
Investment – Money Market	4	120,000	120,000
		126,812	125,000
TOTAL ASSETS		$282,772	$324,821
REPRESENTED BY:			
EQUITY AND LIABILITIES			
Accumulated Fund		165,304	147,657
CURRENT LIABILITIES			
Bank Overdraft		-	100,000
Directors Account	5	117,468	77,194
		117,468	177,194
TOTAL EQUITY AND LIABILITIES		$282,772	$324,851

The notes and schedules on pages 6 to 10 form part of these financial statements

On the 13th March, 2025, the Board of Directors of Mobak Foundation authorized these financial statements for issue.

PRESIDENT... SECRETARY..

TREASURER...

2.

MOBAK FOUNDATION
STATEMENT OF COMPREHENSIVE INCOME
FOR THE YEAR ENDED
31ST DECEMBER, 2021

	SCHEDULES	2021	2020
INCOME			
Subscriptions & Donations		200,500	537,234
EXPENSES			
General and Administrative	1	55,156	136,582
MOBAK Transitional Programme	2	53,500	181,739
MOBAK Help Programme		30,000	10,000
MOBAK Grant		-	30,000
MOBAK Farms		-	6,575
MOBAK Community Events		-	20,500
Interest and Bank Charges		306	750
Depreciation		43,891	57,345
		182,853	443,491
NET SURPLUS		$17,647	$93,743

The notes and schedules on pages 6 to 10 form part of these financial statements

MOBAK FOUNDATION
STATEMENT OF CHANGES IN EQUITY
FOR THE YEAR ENDED
31ST DECEMBER, 2021

	2021
AS AT 31ST DECEMBER, 2021	
Accumulated Fund at 1.1	147,657
Surplus for the Year	17,647
Accumulated Fund at 31.12	$165,304

AS AT 31ST DECEMBER, 2020	**2020**
Accumulated Fund at 1.1	53,914
Surplus for the Year	93,743
Accumulated Fund at 31.12	$147,657

The notes and schedules on pages 6 to 10 form part of these financial statements

MOBAK FOUNDATION
STATEMENT OF CASH FLOW
FOR THE YEAR ENDED
31ST DECEMBER, 2021

OPERATING ACTIVITIES	**2021**
Profit for the Year	17,647
Adjustments for non-cash items	
Depreciation	43,891
Operating Profit after Working Capital Changes	61,538
Changes in Operating Assets and Liabilities	
Increase in Current Liabilities	40,274
Cash (used) provided by Operating Activities	101,812
INVESTING ACTIVITIES	
Cash used in Investing Activities	-
FINANCING ACTIVITIES	
Cash used in Financing Activities	-
Net Increase in Cash and Cash Equivalents	101,812
Cash at 1.1	(95,000)
Cash at 31.12	$6,812
REPRESENTED BY:	
Cash on Hand and at Bank	$6,812

The notes and schedules on pages 6 to 10 form part of these financial statements

STATEMENT OF FINANCIAL POSITION

As 31st December

	Notes	2022	2021
NON-CURRENT ASSETS	1		
Lease Property		1,000,000	0
Office Furniture & Fittings		8,072	9,225
Gym Equipment		22,068	0
Office Equipment		12,320	15,680
Motor Vehicles		110,000	110,000
Books		3,580	3,580
Total Non-Current Assets		**1,156,040**	**138,485**
CURRENT ASSETS			
Investment – Money market		120,000	120,000
Directors Account		**0**	337,159
Cash and Bank		1,748	6,812
Total Current Assets		**121,748**	**463,971**
TOTAL ASSETS		**1,277,788**	**602,456**
EQUITY AND LIABILITIES			
EQUITIES			

Exercise 19

What is the difference between a Receipt and Payments Account and an Income and Expenditure Account.

Exercise 20 - Quiz

Nos	Statements	True	False
	The church does not operate with a profit-making motive as a trading business, but must account for monies received and monies spent		
	The budget and budgeting are unnecessary in the administration of cash resources		
	A financial transaction is an agreement or a communication between a buyer and seller to exchange goods and services or assets for payment		
	A church need not record all its financial transactions		
	Financial Records in a business are kept in main 'books or systems that keep Cash, ledger and minor "books' e.g. Sales, Purchases		
	The Cash Book is the main book of record for the church		
	The church should do all its financial business in cash		
	The pastor must always be one of the signatories of cheques		
	A Bank Reconciliation Statement seeks to reconcile the differences between the balance as be cash book and that of the bank statement		
	A payment voucher must be prepared and approved before any payment is made		
	All financial transactions must have documentary support		
	The church financial records must be kept safely at the Treasurer' home		
	The pastor and church leaders must give financial reports to the church members		
	Regulations and statutory requirements require the church to present financial statements which are different in formats than those of a business, albeit the contents are similar		
	The church can however prepare accounts such as Receipt and Payments and Income and Expenditure, especially for internal use		
	The difference between the total money received and total monies spent is called Balance		
	Deficit in the Income and Expenditure account is where the income is more than the expenditure		
	It is OK for the same person who counts the money, to make the entries in the books, to deposit the money in the bank and to prepare the Financial Report		

Summary

Church accounting or the administration of cash is the specialized process of managing a church's finances in a way that is transparent, responsible, and aligned with both spiritual and legal obligations. It differs from for-profit accounting in several keyways, primarily because churches are nonprofit, donor-funded entities.

The Budget is a cost plan for a specific period e.g. monthly, quarterly or annually. It is also a road map. The required steps in the budgeting process therefore include

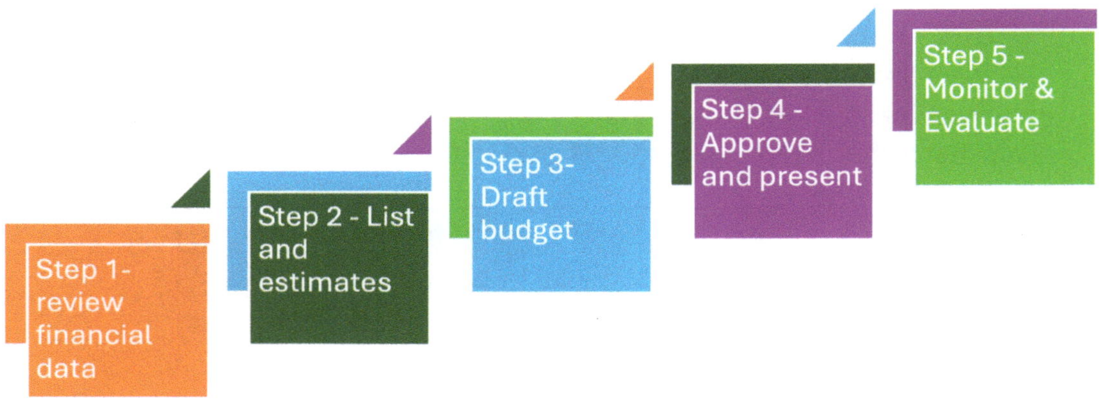

Financial transactions are those that have to do with the exchange of money for goods and services. Hence, they are to be recorded systematically and in accordance with generally accepted accounting standards. For the church however the main "book" for the record of the financial transactions will be the Cash Book

The Bank Reconciliation Statement is a statement that seeks to reconcile and/or explain the balance as per cash book and the balance as per bank statement. The church then must prepare such a statement at least monthly.

Whereas the church is required to prepare financial statements in accordance with what is expected of a non-profit organisation, for internal use it can prepare and use such statements as Receipts & Payments and Income & Expenditure Statements.

Chapter 6

Administration of Events

Objective

Event management is the process of planning and executing an event or an entire event programme, from the beginning stages of planning to post-event reporting. Some understand this and have had successful events. Others do not.

This chapter therefore is to enable those in events to do better, and more successfully.

Approach

Examinations will be made under the following captions:

- Planning the event
- Promotion of the event
- Performance of the event
- Post examination of the event

Two 01st day of the week ago, otherwise called Sundays, I was at a church, and heard the announcement given. The person took about 30 minutes. This was not because the person was a slow reader but because there were so many events that the church had set itself to do in the coming week and beyond.

Every week the church is engaged in events. But there are many cases to show that most of these events could have been done better and could have been more successful,

Success or failure may well have occurred because answers to the following questions were not carefully and prayerfully addressed:

1. How much planning was done for each event?
2. What is the expected outcome or goal of each event?
3. Who is the target audience?
4. What is the budget?
5. What is the programme for the event?
6. How much of that plan would be from the beginning of the event to the post reporting
7. Was there clarity with respect of the event –scope, size, type, in-person, virtual
8. Was each event broken down in parts with an approach assigned to each part

9. How much attention was given to promotion, funding and other required resources

The approach then to the administration of Events are shown in Diagram 32 below:

Diagram 32: EVENTS MANAGEMENT

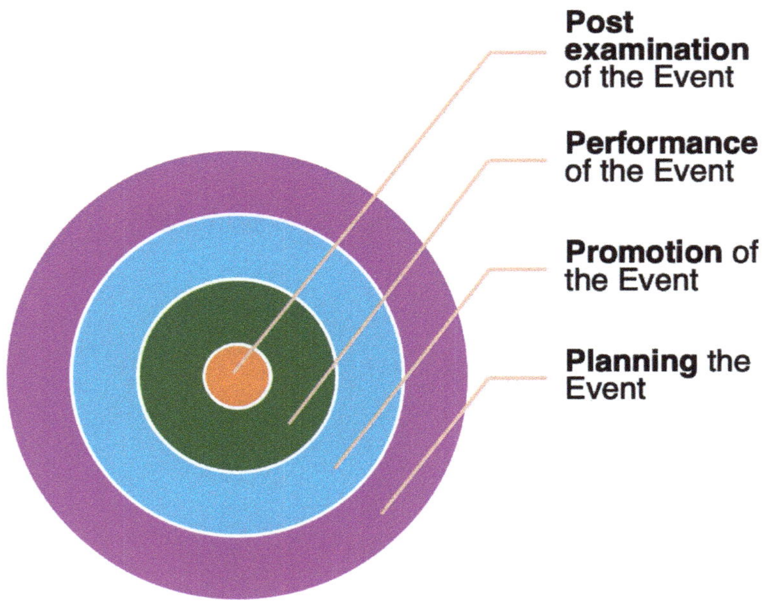

1. **Planning the event**

Event planning is the process of organizing and coordinating all the details necessary to create a successful gathering, celebration or meeting, It involves everything from setting objectives, choosing a date and a venue, arranging logistics, and coordinating entertainment to managing budgets, timelines and guest lists. Careful planning ensures a seamless, enjoyable experience for all involved.

It is recommended that events planned be done by a committee with a capable person to be the Head. It is further recommended there be on the Committee people who would have experience and skills in event management. The same could include planning and organizing, programme designing, budgeting, communication, negotiation, and problem-solving

At the planning meetings, agreements must be made with respect to a wide range of issues and plans to take the required actions. Some of the issues will include intended outcomes or goals, date, time and location of the event and the budget. See Exercise below

Exercise 21

You and your team have planned an open-air meeting. Complete the following, therefore.

Date................................Time...........................Location........................

Nos	Planning Items	Planned actions	Responsible
	The Event		
	Expected outcome		
	Targeted audience		
	Resources: Bible tracts, cards, equipment		
	Music		
	Budgeted amount		
	Speaker		
	Counsellors		
	Theme		
	Music		
	Transport		

2. **Promoting the event**.

Conclusively, Promoting the event is using a marketing tool to communicate with an audience and to convince and influence that audience about the product or service that a customer is gained.

Marketing also teaches that the following are the various types of promotion

Advertising- it reaches a mass of people in a few seconds via radio, television, outdoor advertising, newspaper or social media, and websites.

Direct Promotion-directly communicates with its customers via. email marketing, text messaging, websites, fliers, online adverts, promotional letters, catalog distributors, etc.

Sales Promotion-a marketing tool to increase sales.

Self-promotion agents directly to the customers to pitch for their product or service.

Public Relation-to broadcast the information or message between a company (NGO, Government agency, business), an individual or a public.

Online Promotion-This includes almost all the elements of the promotion mix.

Exercise 22

You and the Events Committee are planning a programme to celebrate the 10th Anniversary of the leadership of the Pastor. Detail the approach you will take, including how the event will be promoted.

Exercise 23

Identify the strengths and weaknesses of the following advertisement.

3. **Performance of the event.**

A business uses several means to measure its successes or failures. The same will include sales, profit, customer satisfaction and liquidity.

In the church however, the measuring tools will be different How is performance measured in the church? Consider the following:

Exercise 24 – Case Study

Evaluation Questionnaire

You are a member of an Event Committee in your church and/or a leader. Your committee planned and executed a recent church event [e.g. family day, a conference, a prayer and fast session, a youth service etc.]. Use the Questionnaire below to evaluate that event.

Nos	Questions	Yes	No
	Were the objectives of the event clearly stated and understood?		
	Would you say that the purpose of the event was realised		
	Were you satisfied with the attendance and participation		
	Were there any decisions to follow Christ or rededications?		
	Were there reports of spiritual growth, encouragement, or conviction?		
	Were there encouraging feedback from the attendees?		
	Were there any standout moments or testimonies?		
	Was there good volunteer turnout and morale?		
	Did the team work well together, and did they feel supported and appreciated?		
	Did the event run smoothly (on time, well-organized, safe)?		
	Were resources (space, equipment, food, etc.) managed effectively?		
	Were there next steps for attendees (e.g., joining a small group, follow-up meetings)?		
	Did the event open doors for further ministry or relationship-building?		
	Did the event stay within budget?		
	Was the financial goal met?		
	Did the event attract new visitors or unchurched individuals?		
	Was there meaningful engagement with the broader community?		

Any other comments

Exercise 25 – Case Study

In a small community village of less than 2,000 persons, he is the pastor of a church that can accommodated 100 members. But for the past three years the average attendance has been 10 people. He is concerned. He attended a church growth conference where among other things he was advised to set goals and to measure the progress being made, Among the goals and measures were:

• Attendance • Membership rolls • Salvations and follow-ups • Outreach programs	• Baptisms • Tithes and giving • Discipleship

He left the conference somewhat dissatisfied. He had looked at all those areas before. He was not too sure that the scriptures were not telling him something different. i.e. Faithfulness, obedience and character are the performance criteria.

2 Corinthians 10:12 [Easy-to-Read Version]

We don't dare put ourselves in the same class as those who think they are so important. We don't compare ourselves to them. They use themselves to measure themselves, and they judge themselves by what they themselves are. This shows that they know nothing.

Acts 2:42-47 [Easy-to-Read Version]

42 *The believers spent their time listening to the teaching of the apostles. They shared everything with each other. They ate[a] together and prayed together.*

43 *Many wonders and miraculous signs were happening through the apostles, and everyone felt great respect for God.*

44 *All the believers stayed together and shared everything.*

45 *They sold their land and the things they owned. Then they divided the money and gave it to those who needed it.*

46 *The believers shared a common purpose, and every day they spent much of their time together in the Temple area. They also ate together in their homes. They were happy to share their food and ate with joyful hearts.*

47 *The believers praised God and were respected by all the people. More and more people were being saved every day, and the Lord was adding them to their group.*

2 Corinthians 13:5 [Easy-to-Read Version]

[5] *Look closely at yourselves. Test yourselves to see if you are living in the faith. Don't you realize that Christ Jesus is in you? Of course, if you fail the test, he is not in you.*

HOW WILL YOU ADVISE THIS PASTOR?

4. **Post-examination of the event**

In 2024, my wife and I attended and participated in an event which could be described as a big one.

The halls were overflowing with participants

- The presentations made were uplifting
- The atmosphere was welcoming
- There was no distraction and/or interruption in the smooth flow of things

Some days after, we met one of the planners and asked whether there will be a post-examination of the event. He assured us that there will be. None occurred.

The point is as good as an event appeared to have been made, there is always a need for a post-examination. That is an activity that seeks to understand and measure the extent to which an event has succeeded in achieving its purpose, goal or expected outcome.

Example of a post-examination [Source: ChatGPT]

A church can conduct a **post-examination (or post-event evaluation)** of an event through a structured process designed to assess effectiveness, identify areas of improvement, and ensure accountability. Here's a step-by-step guide to how a church might do this:

1. **Schedule a Debrief Meeting**

- **Timing:** Within a few days to a week after the event.
- **Participants:** Key organizers, volunteers, ministry leaders, and possibly attendees (via feedback).
- **Goal:** Create a safe space for honest discussion.

2. **Review Objectives and Outcomes**

- **Compare planned goals** with actual results.
- **Questions to ask:**
    - What was the event's purpose (spiritual, outreach, fundraising, fellowship)?
    - Were attendance and engagement levels as expected?
    - Did it stay within budget?

3. **Collect and Review Feedback**

- **Sources:**

- Attendee surveys (paper or digital)
    - Verbal feedback
    - Volunteer feedback
    - Social media responses
- **Feedback should cover:**
    - Logistics (venue, time, flow)
    - Worship or speaker sessions
    - Hospitality and atmosphere
    - Spiritual impact

4. **Analyze What Went Well**

- Identify **successes**:
    - High attendance?
    - Spiritual impact?
    - Strong teamwork?
    - Smooth logistics?

5. **Identify Challenges or Issues**

- Be honest about:
    - Logistical problems
    - Communication gaps
    - Volunteer burnout
    - Low engagement in parts of the event

6. **Document Lessons Learned**

- Write a **summary report** including:
    - What worked well
    - What could improve
    - Quotes or testimonies
    - Metrics (budget, Attendance, etc.)

7. **Make Recommendations**

- Suggest **specific changes** for future events.
- Assign responsible persons or teams to follow up on these.

8. **Archive the Report**

- Store the report and resources (photos, videos, budget records) for reference.
- This helps future planning teams avoid repeating mistakes.

Exercise 26

The annual church dinner was recently held. But many of the attendees complained.

The programme started late

- Those who were in charge were shoddy and sloppy
- The food was not up to standard
- The atmosphere was unfriendly and unwelcoming
- How will you and your Planning Committee treat these complaints?

Summary

Event management is the process of planning and executing an event or an entire event programme, from the beginning stages of planning to post-event reporting.

The administration of church events has been considered under the following captions:

- Planning the event
- Promotion of the event
- Performance of the event
- Post examination of the event

Planning the event is the process of organizing and coordinating all the details necessary to create a successful gathering, celebration or meeting,

Promoting the event.is using a marketing tool to communicate with an audience and to convince and influence that audience about the product or service that a customer is gained.

The performance of the event can be measured by several means.

Post-examination of an event is an activity that seeks to understand and measure the extent to which that event has succeeded in achieving its purpose, goal or expected outcome.

Chapter 7

Administration of Services

Objective

A church offers a wide range of services to its members. These include spiritual, educational, fellowship and administration. But Mathew 25:31-46 and other scriptures show that the church also ought to provide community and social services as well. Interestingly members benefit from these services.

This Chapter explores these community and social services so that the administration of them can be better addressed.

Approach

These community and social services of the church are considered under the following:

1. Feeding the hungry
2. Giving drinks to the thirsty
3. caring for the homeless
4. welcoming the immigrants
5. clothing the naked
6. Caring for the sick
7. Visiting the imprisoned

Starpoint – Mathew 25:31-39 [Easy-to-Read Version]

31 *"The Son of Man will come again with divine greatness, and all his angels will come with him. He will sit as king on his great and glorious throne.*

32 *All the people of the world will be gathered before him. Then he will separate everyone into two groups. It will be like a shepherd separating his sheep from his goats.*

33 *He will put the sheep on his right and the goats on his left.*

34 *"Then the king will say to the godly people on his right, 'Come, my Father has great blessings for you. The kingdom he promised is now yours. It has been prepared for you since the world was made.*

35 *It is yours because when I was hungry, you gave me food to eat. When I was thirsty, you gave me something to drink. When I had no place to stay, you welcomed me into your home.*

36 *When I was without clothes, you gave me something to wear. When I was sick, you cared for me. When I was in prison, you came to visit me.'*

37 *"Then the godly people will answer, 'Lord, when did we see you hungry and give you food? When did we see you thirsty and give you something to drink?*

38 *When did we see you with no place to stay and welcome you into our home? When did we see you without clothes and give you something to wear?*

39 *When did we see you sick or in prison and care for you?'*

The several interpretations of these verses have in common that serving others is serving Christ. Our treatment of the poor, sick, strangers, and imprisoned reflects our relationship with Him. Table 3 below summarizes some interpretation of these by different traditions.

Table 3: Summary of Comparative interpretation of Mathew 25:31-39

Catholic - Faith and Works

a) Affirmation that salvation involves both faith and work.
b) The Corporal Works of Mercy (feeding the hungry, clothing the naked, visiting the sick, etc.) are grounded here.
c) The importance of charity, social justice, and care for the marginalized

Evangelical Protestant - Faith that Produces Works

a) Salvation is by grace through faith alone (Ephesians 2:8–9).
b) However, genuine saving faith necessarily bears fruit—good works, T.
c) True believers naturally serve others.

Eastern Orthodox - Theosis [Becoming more like God] and Love

a) Love and mercy toward others are participation in the divine life.

Mainline Protestant (e.g., Anglican, Lutheran, Methodist) - Ethical Living, Social Justice

Liberation Theology (re in Latin America) - God's Preferential Option for the Poor

a) radical call to align with the oppressed and marginalized.
b) Serving the "least of these" is seen not only as Christian charity but as justice and solidarity.

Other supporting scriptures

: Hebrews 13:1-5 [Easy-to-Read Version]

1 *Continue loving each other as brothers and sisters in Christ.*

2 *Always remember to help people by welcoming them into your home. Some people*

have done that and have helped angels without knowing it.

[3] *Don't forget those who are in prison. Remember them as though you were in prison with them. And don't forget those who are suffering. Remember them as though you were suffering with them.*

Diagram 33 - Summary

Luke 4:15-22 [Easy-to-Read Version]

16 *Jesus traveled to Nazareth, the town where he grew up. On the Sabbath day he*
went to the synagogue as he always did. He stood up to read.

17 *The book of Isaiah the prophet was given to him. He opened the book and found*
the place where this is written:

18 *"The Spirit of the Lord is on me.*

He has chosen me to tell good news to the poor.

He sent me to tell prisoners that they are free

and to tell the blind that they can see again.

He sent me to free those who have been treated badly

19 *and to announce that the time has come for the Lord to show his kindness."*

20 *Jesus closed the book, gave it back to the helper, and sat down. As everyone in the*
synagogue watched him closely,

21 *he began to speak to them. He said, "While you heard me reading these words just now, they were coming true!"*

Diagram 34- Summary: Social and Community Services

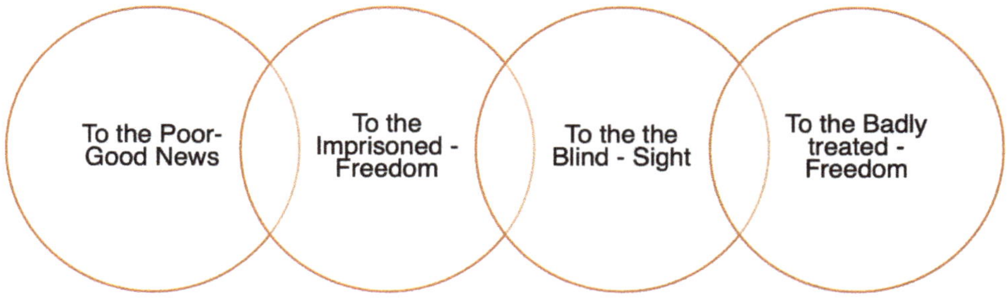

Feeding the hungry

On Sunday 26th May 2025, my family and I left church and were on our way home. But we decided firstly to make some purchases at the nearby market. There however we saw a long line of people being offered food by a Christian group. We were pleased. In fact, I went to the head of the group and thanked him for the services they were providing in feeding the poor and hungry

The following Sunday, we had the same sight in the same market. But this time, it was by another group of Christians. Clearly then the believers in that part of London England have not only understood the spiritual imperative of feeding the poor but also by doing so they express their faith, compassion, and obedience to God.

Overview of Feeding the poor in Christianity [Source ChatGPT]:

1. Biblical Foundations

Old Testament:

- *God's law repeatedly commands care for the poor, including feeding the hungry:*
  - ***Proverbs 19:17**: "Whoever is kind to the poor lends to the Lord, and He will reward them for what they have done."*
  - ***Isaiah 58:6–7**: "Is not this the fast I have chosen... to share your food with the hungry?"*

New Testament:

- *Jesus' teachings center heavily on **compassion for the poor** and marginalized.*

- ***Matthew 25:35***: *"For I was hungry and you gave me something to eat..." — helping the poor is helping Christ Himself.*
- ***James 2:15–17***: *"If a brother or sister is poorly clothed and lacking in daily food... what good is it?" Faith must result in action.*

✝ 2. Jesus and the Poor

- *Jesus **lived among the poor**, fed the hungry (e.g., the feeding of the 5,000), and commanded His followers to care for them.*
- ***Luke 14:13***: *"When you give a feast, invite the poor, the crippled, the lame, the blind..."*
- *He warned against wealth that ignores the needs of the poor (**Luke 16:19–31**, the parable of the rich man and Lazarus).*

🏛 3. The Early Church

- *The Book of Acts records that the early Christians **shared their possessions** to ensure no one was in need (**Acts 4:32–35**).*
- *The apostles prioritized care for widows and the distribution of food (**Acts 6:1–6**).*
- *Paul took up **collections for the poor** (e.g., in Jerusalem), emphasizing unity through generosity (**Romans 15:25–27**).*

🕯 4. Church Tradition and Practice

Catholic and Orthodox Churches:

- *Feeding the poor is one of the **Corporal Works of Mercy** (Catholicism).*
- *Monasteries historically served as centers of hospitality and food distribution.*
- *Lent and other fasting seasons are tied to **giving what you withhold from yourself** to those in need.*

Protestant Churches:

- *Reformers like **Martin Luther and John Wesley** emphasized helping the poor as an outworking of faith.*
- *Many Protestant denominations run **food banks, shelters, and soup kitchens**.*
- *Evangelicals often link feeding the poor with **mission work and discipleship**.*

🌍 5. Modern Christian Response

- *Churches and Christian NGOs around the world—like **World Vision**, **Samaritan's Purse**, **Caritas**, and **The Salvation Army**—are major providers of food aid.*
- *Local congregations frequently run **community meals, food pantries, and holiday meal programs**.*

☑ *Summary: Feeding the Poor in Christianity*

Principle	***Teaching***
Moral duty	*Seen as a core Christian responsibility*
Reflection of Christ	*Serving the poor is serving Jesus Himself*
Faith in action	*Evidence of genuine faith (James 2:17)*
Biblical mandate	*Taught consistently in both Testaments*
Church heritage	*Practiced since the early church*
Global mission	*Integral to Christian humanitarian work*

Caring for the homeless

When I was the Pastor of a NTCG, church in Romford, England, we provided services to the homeless. Interestingly, despite its supposed wealth, the UK has a significant portion of its population that is homeless and does not have food. Every week, we open the church for the homeless. It was winter. We provided warm beds, hot beverages and breakfast for more than 20 people. We also took the opportunity to befriend the homeless and minister God's word to them. That programme was successful. It was our joy therefore that many years after we had moved on from the church, provision was still being made for the homeless. They are not provided with sleeping facilities, but rather they are given hot beverages and sandwiches on a weekly basis.

Immigrants

Immigrants -foreigners, strangers, or sojourners – God is clear in His words on how immigrants are to be treated. His people are to treat them, with justice, compassion, and love—remembering that they, too, were once outsiders.

Note the following:

Exodus 22:21 [21] "You shall neither mistreat a [a] stranger nor oppress him, for you were strangers in the land of Egypt.	Deuteronomy 10:18-19 [18] He administers justice for the fatherless and the widow, and loves the stranger, giving him food and clothing. [19] Therefore love the stranger, for you were strangers in the land of Egypt.

Matthew 25:35 [35] for I was hungry and you gave Me food; I was thirsty and you gave Me drink; I was a stranger, and you took Me in;	Galatians 3:28 [28] There is neither Jew nor Greek, there is neither slave nor free, there is neither male nor female; for you are all one in Christ Jesus

Ephesians 2:19 [19] Now, therefore, you are no longer strangers and foreigners, but fellow citizens with the saints and members of the household of God,	Hebrews 13:2 [2] Do not forget to entertain strangers, for by so *doing* some have unwittingly entertained angels.

The world and world leaders have taken a different position. Theirs is to keep immigrants from coming and/or staying in their countries and mass deporting them. The process is done in the most inhumane and non-compassionate manner.

Table 4 provides the latest policy changes in the UK and USA

Table 4

UK	**USA**
Key Policy Changes: **Visa Restrictions Based on Overstay Rates**: would target individuals using fraudulent documents or posing as destitute to access taxpayer-funded accommodations. **Higher Financial Thresholds**: Beginning January 2, 2025, the UK will enforce higher financial thresholds for immigrants. **Electronic Travel Authorization (ETA)**: The UK has introduced an Electronic Travel Authorization system requiring foreign nationals who intend to visit the United Kingdom without a visa to obtain advance travel permission.	**Key Policy Changes:** **Mass Deportation Funding**: President **Voluntary Self-Deportation Program**: a program offering undocumented immigrants a $1,000 stipend and travel assistance to voluntarily leave the U.S., **Laken Riley Act**: Signed into law on January 29, 2025, this act requires the Department of Homeland Security to detain illegal immigrants admitting to, charged with, or convicted of theft-related crimes, assaulting a police officer, or a crime that results in death or serious bodily injury. **Executive Order 14159**: Titled "Protecting The American People Against Invasion," this order expands expedited removal, denies federal funding to sanctuary jurisdictions, imposes penalties for undocumented immigrants who fail to register, and increases hiring of immigration enforcement agents.

Caring for the sick

Caring for the sick is a central expression of Christian faith, deeply rooted in the life and teachings of Jesus Christ and supported in scriptures and evidenced in both history and current engagement of the church.

Scriptural support

Matthew 8:16-17

16 *When evening had come, they brought to Him many who were demon-possessed.*
And He cast out the spirits with a word, and healed all who were sick, ***17*** *that it might*
be fulfilled which was spoken by Isaiah the prophet, saying:

"He Himself took our infirmities

And bore our sicknesses."

Mark 1:40-42

40 *Now a leper came to Him, imploring Him, kneeling down to Him and saying to Him,*
"If You are willing, You can make me clean."

41 *Then Jesus, moved with compassion, stretched out His hand and touched him, and*
said to him, "I am willing; be cleansed." ***42*** *As soon as He had spoken, immediately*
the leprosy left him, and he was cleansed.

Luke 8:43-48

43 *Now a woman, having a flow of blood for twelve years, who had spent all her*
livelihood on physicians and could not be healed by any, ***44*** *came from behind and*
touched the border of His garment. And immediately her flow of blood stopped.

45 *And Jesus said, "Who touched Me?"*

When all denied it, Peter [a]and those with him said, "Master, the multitudes throng and press You, [b]and You say, 'Who touched Me?' "

46 *But Jesus said, "Somebody touched Me, for I perceived power going out from Me."*

47 *Now when the woman saw that she was not hidden, she came trembling; and falling down before Him, she declared to Him in the presence of all the people the reason she had touched Him and how she was healed immediately.*

48 *And He said to her, "Daughter, [c]be of good cheer; your faith has made you well. Go in peace."*

Table 5 provides more examples of the healing ministry of Jesus Christ

Table 5: Examples of individuals Jesus healed

Nos.	Healing	Reference
1	Man with leprosy	Matthew 8:2–4
2	Centurion's servant	Matthew 8:5–13
3	Peter's mother-in-law	Matthew 8:14–15
4	Paralyzed man lowered through roof	Mark 2:1–12
5	Man with withered hand	Mark 3:1–6
6	Woman with bleeding for 12 years	Mark 5:25–34
7	Jairus' daughter raised (healing/resurrection)	Mark 5:35–43
8	Two blind men	Matthew 9:27–31
9	Mute man possessed by a demon	Matthew 9:32–33
10	Canaanite woman's daughter	Matthew 15:21–28
11	Deaf and mute man	Mark 7:31–37
12	Blind man at Bethsaida	Mark 8:22–26
13	Blind man Bartimaeus	Mark 10:46–52
14	Ten lepers (only one returned to thank Him)	Luke 17:11–19
15	Man born blind	John 9
16	Malchus' ear (during Jesus' arrest)	Luke 22:50–51

Scriptures also show that Jesus did mass healings:

Matthew 4:24

24 Then [a]His fame went throughout all Syria; and they brought to Him all sick people who were afflicted with various diseases and torments, and those who were demon-possessed, epileptics, and paralytics; and He healed them.

Matthew 8:16-17

Luke 6:19

19 And the whole multitude sought to touch Him, for power went out from Him and healed *them* all

The following scriptures are also to be noted:

Acts 3:1-10

1 Now Peter and John went up together to the temple at the hour of prayer, the ninth
hour. 2 And a certain man lame from his mother's womb was carried, whom they laid
daily at the gate of the temple which is called Beautiful, to [a]ask alms from those

who entered the temple; 3 who, seeing Peter and John about to go into the temple,
asked for alms. 4 And fixing his eyes on him, with John, Peter said, “Look at us.” 5 So
he gave them his attention, expecting to receive something from them. 6 Then Peter
said, “Silver and gold I do not have, but what I do have I give you: In the name of
Jesus Christ of Nazareth, rise up and walk.” 7 And he took him by the right hand and
lifted *him* up, and immediately his feet and ankle bones received strength. 8 So he,
leaping up, stood and walked and entered the temple with them—walking, leaping,
and praising God. 9 And all the people saw him walking and praising God. 10 Then they
knew that it was he who sat begging alms at the Beautiful Gate of the temple; and
they were filled with wonder and amazement at what had happened to him.

Acts 9:32-35

32 Now it came to pass, as Peter went through all *parts of the country,* that he also
came down to the saints who dwelt in Lydda. 33 There he found a certain man named
Aeneas, who had been bedridden eight years and was paralyzed. 34 And Peter said to
him, “Aeneas, Jesus the Christ heals you. Arise and make your bed.” Then he arose
immediately. 35 So all who dwelt at Lydda and Sharon saw him and turned to the Lord.

James 5:14-15

14 Is anyone among you sick? Let him call for the elders of the church, and let them
pray over him, anointing him with oil in the name of the Lord. 15 And the prayer of faith
will save the sick, and the Lord will raise him up. And if he has committed sins, he will
be forgiven

My Testimony

I grew up and do believe in the practice of caring for the sick and praying and seeing many healed.

Amari Cumberbatch, one of our seven grandchildren, was born very prematurely. The doctors had concluded that she could not live and even if she lived, she would have physical challenges and be deformed. The church prayed. Her parents and family prayed. Her grandparents prayed.

On January 08th, 2025, Amaris celebrated her 9th birthday. She attends school and is doing well mentally, physically, socially and spiritually.

Secondly, during our pastorate in the UK, our church was engaged in Healing on the Street ministry. This was one where we would go out on the streets and invite persons for prayers for healing. Some came. Some testified to be healed.

Prison Ministry

One of the most challenging experiences we had as a church was in the prison ministry. We did this ministry in the land of my birth, Trinidad and Tobago as well as in the UK.

Crowded in small cells and with little amenities or exercise or fresh air, the prisoners in Trinidad and Tobago were really in prisons. The visits then were not like visiting the sick or feeding the hungry. We were constrained in how physically close we can be to the prisoners; in what we were allowed to give them and even in what we could say to them.

The prisoners were brought out of their cells. They were fitted into one small room, where we would meet and minister to them. At best then we had a "church" service with them. We would give them our names, but never where we lived. The prisons in Trinidad and Tobago do not necessarily reform prisoners. When those prisoners come out of prisons, they can pose a threat to people and their possessions.

In the UK we did prison ministry for many more years. We visited those in high security prisons as well as those in low security prisons. There was also the case of detailed background checks being made on persons who wanted to do prison ministry. I can recall a brother who was debarred because many years before, he was himself a prisoner.

The prison authorities were watchful when the prison ministry was done. Firstly, we were thoroughly checked and searched before we could have entered the prison. Notices were posted everywhere stating in part should one be found bringing in mobile phones or any other prohibited items that person would be arrested and charged.

I recall when we entered HMP Belmarsh the UK, we were checked as if we ourselves were prisoners. Dogs sniffed us. We were figure printed, and body searched. And when we were eventually led into the prison hall and had a one-to-one session with prisoners, the guards stood around paying close attention to what was happening.

His Majesty's Prison Belmarsh is a Category A men's prison in Thamesmead, southeast London, England. Prison is used for high-profile cases, particularly those concerning national security. Within the grounds is the High Security Unit (HSU), which consists of 48 single cells. It is run by His Majesty's Prison Service. The prison has been called "Britain's Guantanamo Bay" due to the long-term detention of terrorism suspects without charge. Considered the toughest prison in the UK, Belmarsh is also notoriously known as "Hellmarsh". Inmates [prisoners] at Belmarsh are offered access to education, workshops and two gyms.

But our most turned off experience however was when we did prison ministry in Brixton. Some inmates who were Muslim complained that we were spreading messages of conversion and the same offended them. The prison authorities asked us to desist from such messages. We ceased doing prison ministry in Brixton.

Exercise 27

Discuss the experience of the church where you are a leader in any of the following services or ministries

- Feeding the hungry
- Caring for the homeless
- Welcoming the immigrants
- Clothing the naked
- Caring for the sick
- Visiting the imprisoned

Summary

A church offers a wide range of services to its members. These include spiritual, educational, fellowship and administration. But Mathew 25:31-46 and other scriptures show that the church also ought to provide community and social services as well. Such services include and are not limited to Feeding the hungry, giving drinks to the thirsty, caring for the homeless, welcoming the immigrants, clothing the naked, caring for the sick, and visiting the imprisoned

Chapter 8

Administration of Statutes

Objective

Church statutes are a written document that outlines the legal identity, purpose, governance, and operating procedures of a church. They are often required by law when registering a church with government authorities (especially in civil law countries like many in Europe, Africa, and parts of Latin America). [ChatGPT]

This Chapter seeks then to examine the statutes of a church so that the administration of them can be better addressed.

Approach

Pursuance of this objective will be made under the following

- Church Constitution, Bylaws, Statutes
- Purpose for statutes of a church
- Content of the statutes of a church
- Preparation of the statues of a church, with Example

Church Constitution, Bylaws, Statutes

These are closely related but not always the same. Diagram 35, Table 6 below sets out the differences.

Diagram 35

Table 6

Church Constitution				
Definition	**Purpose**	**Content**	**Focus**	**Scope**:
The foundational document that outlines the core beliefs, purpose, and governance structure of the church	Sets the broad framework for how the church operates — kind of like a "mission and values" charter	Name, purpose, statement of faith, basic structure of leadership and membership	Purpose, beliefs, structure	Broad, Foundational
Church Bylaws				
Definition	**Purpose**	**Content**	**Focus**	**Scope:**
Detailed rules and procedures for how the church's constitution is applied in day-to-day governance	Outlines the "how" — elections, meetings, roles, finances, membership processes.	Voting rules, officer duties, meeting procedures, how to amend documents, etc	Specific, procedural	Daily operations and rules
Church Statutes				
Definition	**Purpose**	**Content**	**Focus**	**Scope**:
A term often used interchangeably with "bylaws" or "constitution," especially in churches that are registered legal entities	combine both the constitution and bylaws into a single legally recognized document [see details below]	Everything from legal name, purpose, doctrine, and governance to financial rules and dissolution procedures	All structural/ legal elements	Legal and comprehensive

Purpose for Church Statutes

While the New Testament does not contain detailed church statutes and/or bylaws, there are examples of establishing order and structure in the early church. These include and are not limited to:

- appointing elders (Acts 14:23),

- creating a process to distribute food (Acts 6:1-6),
- sending representatives from churches to discuss doctrinal issues (Acts 15:2),
- giving instructions about the Lord's Supper (1 Corinthians 11:2, 17-26),
- approving servants to handle finances (2 Corinthians 8:19).

The extensive regulations given to Old Testament Israel also reinforce the appropriateness of biblical statutes and/or bylaws – God is a God of order. Rules and governing documents protected righteousness and punished wickedness in the nation.

The following therefore are some of the detailed purposes for church statutes and/or bylaws

1. Provide legal recognition and compliance with government regulations and statutory requirements
2. Ensure that the church operates with clarity, order, unity, guidance, accountability and continuity, protection of its resources and policies and procedures - e.g. checks and balances for handling money [2 Corinthians 8:20-21]. Policies for counting, depositing, reporting, authorizing spending, auditing. Wise policies avert confusion and offense that create disunity. Orderly structure and clear process cultivate harmony.
3. Treat with organizational structure, leadership, governance, membership and authority structures, church discipline re Acts, 6:1-6, 20:28, Titus 1:5, Philippians 1:1,1 Peter 5:1-3 and 1 Corinthians 5, Galatians 6:1. While elders lead, the congregation participates in affirming leaders [Acts 14:23,] church discipline [Matthew 18:15-20], doctrinal decisions [Acts 15:22], and financial matters [2 Corinthians 8:19]. Statutes define their role.
4. Regulate church ordinances/practices and anchor the church in biblical truth e.g. baptism and the Lord's Supper, weddings, funerals, child dedications, etc. re 1 Corinthians 11:17-34, 15:1-4, Ephesians 2:8-9, 20, 2 Timothy 3:16, Matthew 28:19.
5. Stipulate procedures for amending governing documents. This prevents confusion and power grabs. Changes are made through defined procedures – often requiring approval by the elders and a congregational vote.

Diagram 36

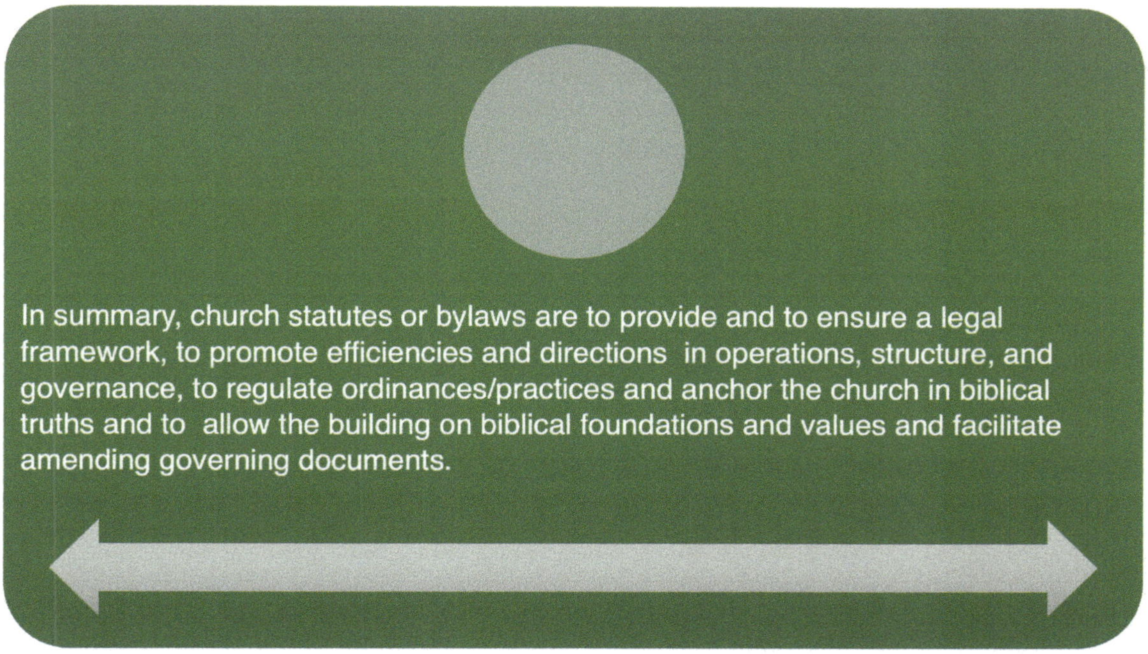

Exercise 28

Complete the following form so as to enable the registration of the church where you attend and are one of the leaders.

CHURCH REGISTRATION FORM

SECTION 1: CHURCH INFORMATION

Proposed Church Name:	....
Physical Address:	....
Mailing Address (if different):	
Phone Number:	....
Email Address:	....
Website (if any)	....
Date Church Was Founded	....

Denominational Affiliation (if any): ....

SECTION 2: LEGAL STRUCTURE

Legal Entity Type: ☐ Religious Organization ☐ Nonprofit Organization ☐ Other:

Country/State of Registration:

Registration Number (if previously registered):

SECTION 3: CHURCH PURPOSE AND ACTIVITIES

Mission Statement:

Primary Activities (check all that apply):

☐ Worship Services

☐ Bible Studies

☐ Community Outreach

☐ Education/Training

☐ Counseling

☐ Youth Programs

☐ Other:

SECTION 4: LEADERSHIP AND GOVERNANCE

Senior Pastor / Lead Minister Name:

Board of Directors or Church Elders:

1. Name: ....Position:.................................
2. Name: .... Position: ....
3. Name: .... Position: ....
4. Name: ....Position:.................................
5. Name: ....Position: ....
6. Name: ....Position: ....
7. Name: ....Position:.................................

Constitution / Bylaws Attached: ☐ Yes ☐ No

SECTION 5: FINANCIAL INFORMATION

Source of Funding: ☐ Donations ☐ Tithes ☐ Grants ☐ Other:

Treasurer's Name:

Annual Budget Estimate (optional):

SECTION 6: REQUIRED ATTACHMENTS

☐ Church Constitution/Bylaws

☐ Statement of Faith

☐ List of Board Members

☐ Proof of Address

☐ Identification Documents of Founders/Leaders

☐ Minutes of Founding Meeting

☐ Certificate of Incorporation (if applicable)

SECTION 7: DECLARATION

We, the undersigned, hereby declare that the information provided above is true and correct to the best of our knowledge, and we seek registration of this church entity under the applicable laws and regulations.

Name [Block]	Position	Signature	Date

Content of the statutes of a church

Exercise 29

List what in your view should be the main areas and/or subject that should be in the statutes or bylaws of a church.

These should be as follows:

1. **Church Identity**
    - Name of the church
    - Location (address)
    - Legal status (nonprofit, religious body)
2. **Mission and Purpose**
    - Religious, educational, or charitable goals
    - Core doctrinal statement or confession of faith
3. **Membership**
    - Who can become a member
    - Rights and obligations of members
    - How membership can end

4. **Leadership and Governance**
    - Offices (pastor, elders, deacons, board)
    - How leaders are appointed or removed
    - Decision-making structures (voting, meetings)
5. **General Assembly/Meetings**
    - Rules for congregational or board meetings
    - How decisions are made and recorded
    - Quorum and voting procedures
6. **Finances and Property**
    - Management of donations, offerings, and assets
    - Budgeting and financial accountability
    - Ownership and use of property
7. **Changes to the Statutes**
    - How the document can be amended
    - Who can propose changes and how they are approved
8. **Dissolution Clause**
    - What happens if the church closes or dissolves
    - Legal transfer of assets (typically to another nonprofit or church)

Exercise 30 – Group Discussion

Establish 4 groups and have each group discuss and report for open discussion, on any of the above subject matter of the Statutes of a church [NB. No group is to choose the same two areas].

Summary

Church statutes are a written document that outlines the legal identity, purpose, governance, and operating procedures of a church. They are often required by law when registering a church with government authorities (especially in civil law countries like many in Europe, Africa, and parts of Latin America). [ChatGPT]

Church Constitution, Bylaws, Statutes are closely related but not always the same. They can be differentiated by way of definition, purpose, content, focus and scope. However, Statutes is a term often used interchangeably with "bylaws" or "constitution,"

Chapter 9

ETHICS

Objective

Ethics *is a system of moral principles. They affect how people make decisions and lead their lives. Ethics is concerned with what is good for individuals and society and is also described as moral philosophy.*

In this context of what is Ethics, consideration will be given to Christian ethics, church ethics, and ministerial ethics. More focus will be given to the latter.

Hence, at the end of this Chapter, participants and readers not only will obtain a clearer understanding and working knowledge of ethics but will be motivated to conduct themselves more ethically.

Approach

1. Ethics
2. Ethical behaviour vs Moral behaviour
3. Christian Ethics, Church Ethics, Ministerial Ethics
4. Key aspects
5. Ethics – The perspective of leading Pastors
6. Ethical Behaviour -Biblical example
7. Ministerial Ethics in the church
8. Misconduct of Ministerial ethics and Restoration
9. Ministerial Code of Ethics

What is Ethics

Many definitions are available. These include but are not limited to the following:

a) **Ethics** *is the study of right and wrong behavior. It deals with the principles that guide how people should act toward others, themselves, and society as a whole. Ethics helps us make decisions that align with values like honesty, fairness, respect, and responsibility*.

b) *Our concepts of ethics have been derived from religions, philosophies and cultures. They infuse debates on topics like abortion, human rights and professional conduct*.

c) *A branch of philosophy* Ethics *is that is responsible for studying the principles that govern the conduct of an individual. Ethical principles depend on the situation in which a person encounters and varies from one individual to another.*

d) *Ethics covers the following dilemmas:*

- *how to live a good life*
- *our rights and responsibilities*
- *the language of right and wrong*
- *moral decisions - what is good and bad?*

From the above therefore, Ethics could be understood as

Diagram 37

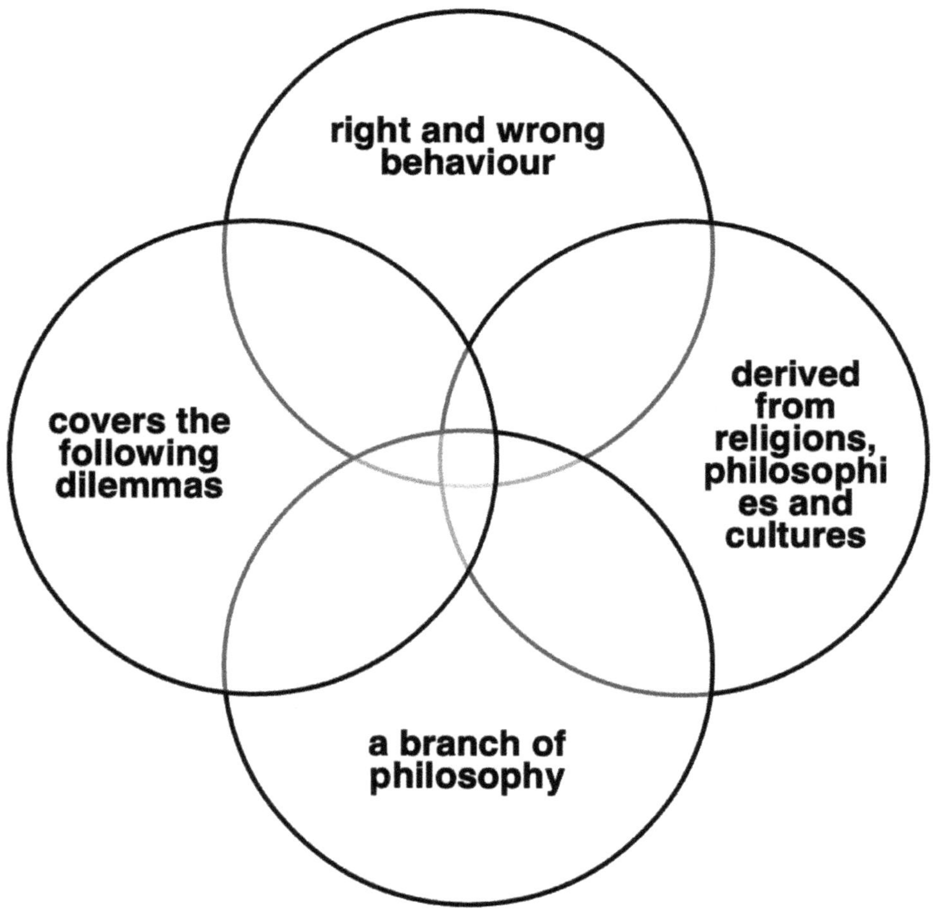

Simply put then Ethics is about knowing the difference between what you have the right to do and what is the right thing to do.

Ethics vs Morality

Comparatively, Morality refers to a group's cultural and religious beliefs, which determine what is right and what is wrong.

Morality offers a set of rules as to what is right or right for any situation. In this sense, it can be said that what is considered morally correct is not always objectively correct.

Ethical behaviour – Moral behaviour

The word"ethics"comes from the Greek *Ethikos,* which means character. The word "moral "comes from the Greek word *Mos, w*hich means custom.

Hence, Diagram 38 and Table 7 below contrast ethical behaviour with moral behaviour

Diagram 38

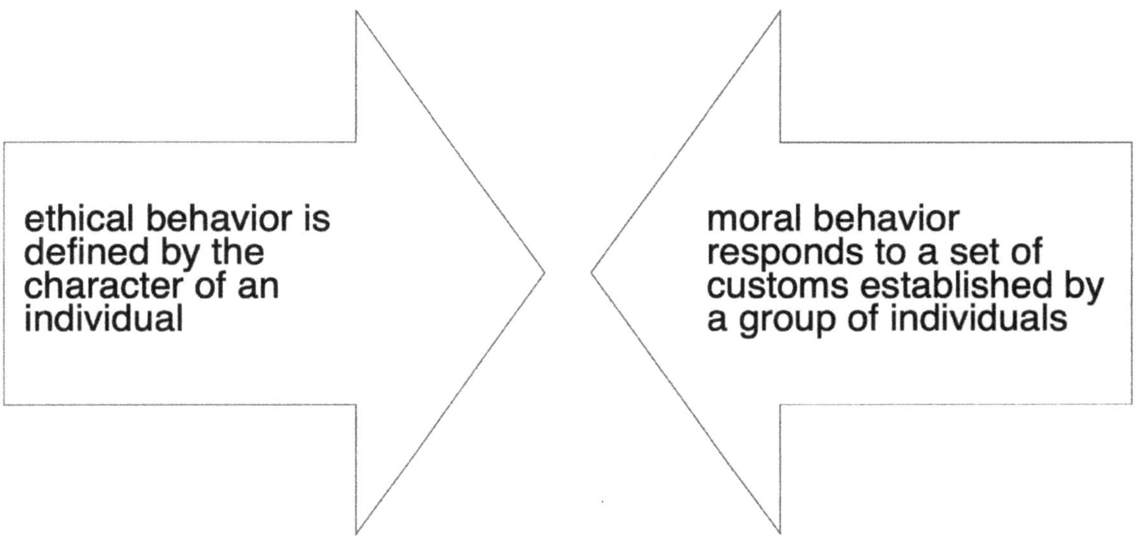

Table 7

Ethical behavior	Moral behavior
An honest person does what he/ she says and does not try to take advantage of others. His/her characteristics include Being charitable Compassionate Respectful	Responses to Exodus 20:13-16 *You shall not murder.* *You shall not commit adultery.* *You shall not steal.* *You shall not bear false witness against your neighbor.*

Examples – Ethical behavior

a) In your village, lives a family that is unable to have food on a daily basis. Every 07th day of the week, otherwise called Saturday, therefore, you provide that family with a hot meal

b) You are selling an item to a customer. After the customer pays, he forgot the purchases and walked away. You immediately run after the customer and give him/her his purchased items.

c) You find on the street a bag of money. You immediately took it up and carried it to a nearby police station.

Exercise 31

Given then the above definition and explanation with respect to what is Ethics, how would you define and/or explain what is

- Christian [Biblical] Ethics
- Church Ethics
- Ministerial Ethics

Christian [Biblical] ethics

The word ethics will not be found in the Bible. But the Bible teaches principles of ethics i.e. how people *ought* to live considering God's character and commands. Biblical ethics are grounded in God's holiness, love, justice, and truth, and are meant to shape how we live, treat others, and serve in ministry.

Hence Christian [Biblical] ethics can be described as the study and practice of how Christians should live according to the moral teachings of the Bible and the example of Jesus Christ. It involves applying biblical principles to guide decision-making and behavior in all areas of life—personal, social, and spiritual

The following scriptures provide some support for the above:

Micah 6:8

"He has shown you, O man, what is good; and what does the Lord require of you but to do justly, to love mercy, and to walk humbly with your God?"

Matthew 22:37–40

"Love the Lord your God with all your heart... and love your neighbor as yourself. All the Law and the Prophets hang on these two commandments."

Romans 12:9–21

"Let love be genuine. Abhor what is evil; hold fast to what is good... Live in harmony... Do not be overcome by evil but overcome evil with good."

Galatians 5:22–23

"But the fruit of the Spirit is love, joy, peace, patience, kindness, goodness, faithfulness, gentleness, and self-control..."

Church ethics refers to the moral principles and values that guide the behavior, decisions, and practices of individuals and organizations within a Christian church context. It is closely tied to Christian [Biblical] ethics, but it focuses more specifically on how these principles apply to church life, including leadership, relationships, governance, and community responsibilities.

The following scriptures provide some support for the above:

1 Timothy 3:1–13 – *Qualifications for Church Leaders*

"Now the overseer is to be above reproach, faithful to his wife, temperate, self-controlled, respectable, hospitable, able to teach..."

Titus 1:5–9 – *Elders Must Live Upright Lives*

"An elder must be blameless... not overbearing, not quick-tempered... but hospitable, one who loves what is good..."

Acts 6:1–7 – *Appointment of Deacons*

"Choose seven men from among you who are known to be full of the Spirit and wisdom..."

Matthew 18:15–17 – *Church Discipline and Conflict Resolution*

[15] "Moreover, if your brother sins against you, go and tell him his fault between you
and him alone. If he hears you, you have gained your brother. [16] But if he will not hear,
take with you one or two more, that 'by the mouth of two or three witnesses every
word may be established.' [17] And if he refuses to hear them, tell *it* to the church. But if
he refuses even to hear the church, let him be to you like a heathen and a tax collector

Hence, these verses build a framework for church ethics—guiding how leaders are chosen, how members behave, how conflicts are resolved, and how holiness and love should define the church.

Ministerial ethics is the set of moral principles and professional standards that guide the behavior, conduct, and responsibilities of ministers, pastors, and other religious leaders. It ensures that those in ministry live and serve in a way that reflects the character of Christ and upholds the trust placed in them by God, their congregation, and the wider community.

The following scriptures provide some support for the above

<u>Personal Integrity and Holiness</u>

1 Peter 1:15–16

"But just as he who called you is holy, so be holy in all you do; for it is written: 'Be holy, because I am holy.'"

1 Timothy 4:12

"Set an example for the believers in speech, in conduct, in love, in faith and in purity."

2 Timothy 2:21–22

"Those who cleanse themselves... will be instruments for special purposes, made holy, useful to the Master..."

<u>Qualifications for Church Leaders</u>

1 Timothy 3:1–13

"Now the overseer is to be above reproach, faithful to his wife... not given to drunkenness... not a lover of money..."

Titus 1:5–9

"He must be blameless... not overbearing or quick-tempered... but one who loves what is good..."

Faithfulness in Teaching and Preaching

2 Timothy 2:15

"Do your best to present yourself to God as one approved... who correctly handles the word of truth."

Titus 2:7–8

"In everything set them an example by doing what is good. In your teaching show integrity...".

<u>Servanthood and Humility</u>

Mark 10:43–45

"Whoever wants to become great among you must be your servant..."

John 13:14–15

"Now that I, your Lord and Teacher, have washed your feet, you also should wash one another's feet."

<u>Accountability and Discipline</u>

James 3:1

"Not many of you should become teachers... because you know that we who teach will be judged more strictly."

1 Corinthians 9:27

"I strike a blow to my body... so that after I have preached to others, I myself will not be disqualified."

Ethical Relationships and Conduct

1 Thessalonians 2:10–12

"You are witnesses... how holy, righteous and blameless we were among you..."

Philippians 2:3–4

"Do nothing out of selfish ambition... in humility value others above yourselves."

Stewardship and Financial Ethics

2 Corinthians 8:20–21

"We are taking pains to do what is right, not only in the eyes of the Lord but also in the eyes of man."

1 Peter 5:2–3

"Be shepherds of God's flock... not pursuing dishonest gain, but eager to serve..."

Conclusively, the above scriptures establish a firm biblical foundation for **ministerial ethics.** Those then who serve who serve God's people do so with

Diagram 39

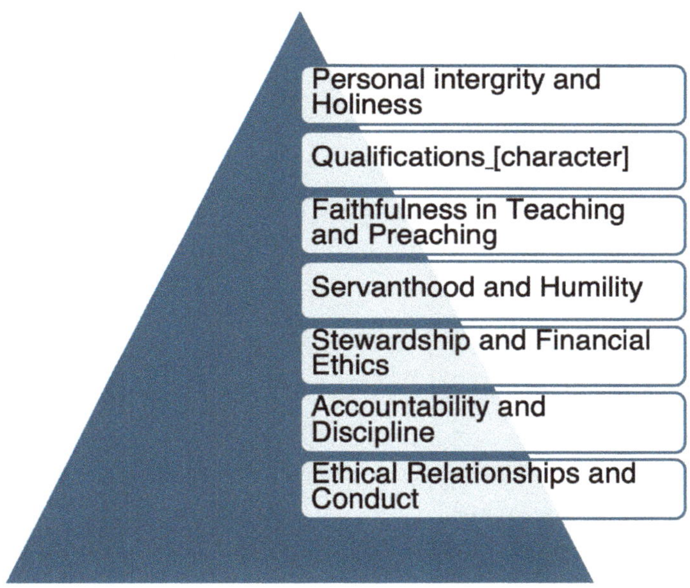

Exercise 32

Take any three verses given above with respect to ministerial ethics and explain how you have applied them in your ministry.

Table 8: Summary of Key Aspects

Ethics	Christian Ethics	Church Ethics	Ministerial Ethics
about doing the right thing, especially when facing difficult decisions	answer the question: "How should a follower of Christ live? • Love (Agape) • Imitation Christ • The Ten Commandments	about practicing what is preached reflecting the character of Christ and the teachings of the Bible.	about character, conduct, and calling—how a minister represents Christ faithfully in public and private life
Moral Principles e.g. *honesty, justice, kindness* :. Right vs. Wrong: *based on reason, conscience, laws, or cultural values* Sources of Ethics: - *Philosophy, religion, culture, norms*	• The Beatitudes • The Fruit of the Spirit • Justice and Mercy • Sanctity of Life • Stewardship • Community and Forgiveness	• Moral Behavior in the Church Community: -, • Ethical Leadership: • Justice, Fairness: • Conflict Resolution: • addressing disagreements • witness to the world	• Personal Integrity • Confidentiality • Accountability • Avoiding Abuse of Power • Relationships • Financial Integrity: • Doctrinal Honesty: • Respect for Other Ministries

Exercise 33

What Ethics is shown in the following situations

Nos	Situations	Christian	Church	Ministerial
1	A and B are both members of the same church. B said bad things about A however, but A forgave him.			
2	Focus includes the love of God and love of one's neighbor			
3	Ethical living happens in community; forgiveness, reconciliation, and peace-making are emphasized (Matthew 18:21–22).			
4	The Pastor did not reveal to the members that he had stolen money from the bank account of the church			
5	Christians are called to follow the example of Jesus in humility, compassion, truthfulness, and obedience to God.			
6	A member of the church told the Pastor of some of the hidden secrets in her life. The Pastor told his wife and another member of the church however			
7	The leaders of the church conducted themselves in accordance with 1 Timothy 3 and Titus 1.			
8	Ethical behavior includes qualities like love, joy, peace, patience, kindness, goodness, faithfulness, gentleness, and self-control			
9	John, a member of the church, had fallen from grace and committed a grievous sin. The members of the church were compassionate to him however.			
10	C started a church in his village. He acts in a manner however to suggest that he is not accountable to the members.			
11	Many persons in that church, including the members say that Pastor C is not a humble person.			
12	Christians are called to responsibly care for God's creation and use resources wisely.			

Nos	Situations	Christian	Church	Ministerial
13	The Pastor twists the truth of Scripture for personal agenda or popularity.			
14	A conflict arose in the church between the 2 members. The Pastor dealt with the conflict as per Mathew 18:15-17			
15	Sanctity of Life			
16	The leadership of the church made Ethical use of resources, time, and talents of the church for the glory of God and the good of the community			
17	The Pastor has compromised his relationships with congregants, colleagues, and family members and shows favoritism, or impropriety			
18	The Pastor at church D, always ensures that proper financial accounts are maintained and financial reports are given.			
19	Consideration is given to Justice and Mercy			
20	The Pastor collaborates with, rather than competes against, other ministers and churches			
21	Using church resources (time, money, property) responsibly and for the mission of the church.			
22	Caring for the environment and using natural resources wisely and ethically			
23	Standing against oppression, helping the marginalized, and promoting fairness in society.			

Diagram 40: Summary: Ethics – Christian, Church, Ministerial

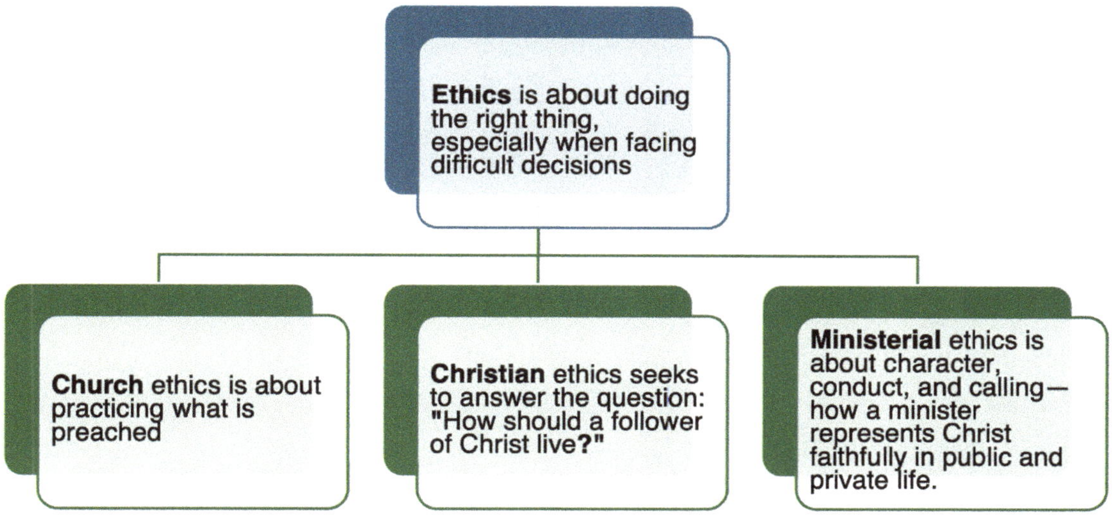

Ethics – The perspective of leading Pastors

Exercise 34

Do you agree with the following statements on Ethics [Christian, Church, Ministerial]

Nos	Statements	Yes	No
1	holiness and righteousness as key attributes of any church worker		
2	Ethics is Living a Christlike Life		
3	Ethics is Living by the Word and Spirit		
4	Ethics is Integrity, Holiness, and Righteousness		
5	Ethics is Integrity, Holiness, and Accountability		
7	"You cannot carry God's power without God's purity."		
8	Nothing works without discipline; destiny is at the mercy of character."		
9	*Pastors must live what they preach, ensuring that their personal lives and ministries align with biblical values.*		
10	*Holiness and Righteous Living: sin, greed, and corruption destroy ministries and that leaders must live above reproach (Hebrews 12:14).*		

Prophet T.B. Joshua *(Synagogue Church of All Nations - SCOAN)*

Ethical Emphasis:

1. *He strongly condemned corruption, greed, and immorality in the church.*
2. *He emphasized holiness and righteousness as key attributes of any church worker.*
3. *His popular phrase "Christianity is not a religion; it is a relationship" highlights his belief that ethical church leadership stems from a personal relationship with Jesus Christ.*
4. *He warned against false prophets and manipulation of church members for financial gain.*

Ethical Quote: "Let love lead."

Dr. Paul Enenche *(Dunamis International Gospel Centre)*

Ethics is Integrity, Holiness, and Righteousness

A strong advocate of moral purity, holiness, and godly character, he teaches that include:

- *Integrity in Ministry: Leaders should be honest, truthful, and free from financial misconduct, deception, or manipulation.*
- *Holiness and Righteous Living: He teaches that sin, compromise, and worldliness must be avoided in ministry (Hebrews 12:14).*
- *Moral Purity: He warns against sexual immorality, greed, and pride, which have destroyed many ministries.*

Ethical Emphasis:

- Strongly preaches against corruption, immorality, and compromise in the pulpit.
- Promotes integrity, hard work, and fearless truth-telling from the pulpit.
- Calls for holiness, justice, and national righteousness.
- Advocates ethical leadership in both the church and society.

Ethical Stand: "You cannot carry God's power without God's purity."

Pastor Chris Oyakhilome *(Christ Embassy / LoveWorld)*

Ethics is Living by the Word and Spirit

- *Integrity and holiness: Church leaders and workers must live by biblical values, avoiding corruption, dishonesty, or manipulation.*
- *Financial transparency: The church should handle finances ethically, ensuring accountability in offerings and donations.*

Bishop David Oyedepo (Living Faith Church / Winners' Chapel)

*Ethical Emphasis:

- Teaches strongly on covenant living, financial integrity, and discipline.

- Promotes a life of excellence, obedience to divine principles, and submission to authority.
- Advocates for ministerial accountability, boldness in faith, and ethical prosperity.
- Criticized by some for strong prosperity teachings but emphasizes stewardship and kingdom service.

Ethical Value: "Nothing works without discipline; destiny is at the mercy of character."

Pastor E.A. Adeboye *(Redeemed Christian Church of God - RCCG)*

**Ethics is Holiness, Integrity, and Accountability*

- Holiness is Non-Negotiable – Leaders must be examples of righteousness and holiness, avoiding corruption, greed, and immorality (Hebrews 12:14).
- Integrity in Ministry – Pastors must live what they preach, ensuring that their personal lives and ministries align with biblical values.
- Financial Integrity – No financial mismanagement, emphasizing accountability and transparency in church finances.
- Moral Purity – No sexual immorality and other ethical failures that can destroy a leader's credibility.
- Obedience to God's Word – Ethical decisions should always be based on biblical principles, not societal trends.

Ethical Behaviour -Biblical examples

From the Bible can be found the following who are exemplars of ethical behavior. They lived with integrity, followed God's commands, and stood for justice and righteousness even in difficult circumstances.

1. Joseph (Genesis 37–50)
    - Ethical traits: Integrity, forgiveness, purity.
    - Example: Refused to commit adultery with Potiphar's wife and later forgave his brothers who sold him into slavery.
2. Daniel (Book of Daniel)
    - Ethical traits: Faithfulness, courage, honesty.
    - Example: Chose to follow God's dietary laws and continued to pray to God despite the threat of death.
3. Ruth (Book of Ruth)
    - Ethical traits: Loyalty, kindness, faithfulness.
    - Example: Stayed with her mother-in-law Naomi and worked hard to provide for her, showing strong family and moral responsibility.
4. Jesus Christ (Gospels)

- Ethical traits: Love, humility, truthfulness, justice.
- Example: Taught and lived by the highest moral standards, loving even enemies, healing the sick, and ultimately sacrificing Himself for others.

5. Job (Book of Job)
   - Ethical traits: Patience, faith, righteousness.
   - Example: Maintained his integrity and trust in God despite severe suffering and loss.
6. Nehemiah (Book of Nehemiah)
   - Ethical traits: Leadership, responsibility, justice.
   - Example: Governed with fairness, rejected personal gain, and helped rebuild Jerusalem while confronting corruption.
7. Samuel (1 Samuel)

Ethical traits: Obedience, integrity, impartiality.

Example: Served as a prophet and judge without abusing power and maintained a clean record of service.

1 Samuel 12:1-4

> 1 *Now Samuel said to all Israel: "Indeed I have [a]heeded your voice in all that you said to me, and have made a king over you.*
>
> 2 *And now here is the king, walking before you; and I am old and grayheaded, and look, my sons are with you. I have walked before you from my childhood to this day.*
>
> 3 *Here I am. Witness against me before the Lord and before His anointed: Whose ox have I taken, or whose donkey have I taken, or whom have I cheated? Whom have I oppressed, or from whose hand have I received any bribe with which to blind my eyes? I will restore it to you.*
>
> 4 *And they said, "You have not cheated us or oppressed us, nor have you taken anything from any man's hand."*

Paul's ethical behaviour

His manner of preaching was free of guile, deceit, flattery, and covetousness. There was no trick involved, no catch, no hidden clause or fine print. Such ethical behaviour was even more essential as in the first century world in which Paul lived, there were many competing religions, and many ministers of those religions were motivated by greed and gain.

Hence in his ministry Paul sought not the glory of men, but of God. He spoke with boldness despite conflict and was gentle and humble among the believers at Thessalonia. His motives were pure. He was as a nursing mother would be with her own children. His manner of life was sacrificial, working hard not to be a burden to them, behaving devoutly, justly, and blamelessly while among them. As a father does his own children, he exhorted, comforted and charged them to walk in a way worthy of God who was calling them into His own kingdom and glory,

References

1 Thessalonians 2 [NKJV]

1 *For you yourselves know, brethren, that our coming to you was not in vain.*

2 *But [a]even after we had suffered before and were spitefully treated at Philippi, as you know, we were bold in our God to speak to you the gospel of God in much conflict.*

3 *For our exhortation did not come from error or uncleanness, nor was it in deceit.*

4 *But as we have been approved by God to be entrusted with the gospel, even so we speak, not as pleasing men, but God who tests our hearts.*

5 *For neither at any time did we use flattering words, as you know, nor a [b]cloak for covetousness—God is witness.*

6 *Nor did we seek glory from men, either from you or from others, when we might have made demands as apostles of Christ.*

7 *But we were gentle among you, just as a nursing mother cherishes her own children.*

8 *So, affectionately longing for you, we were well pleased to impart to you not only the gospel of God, but also our own lives, because you had become dear to us.*

9 *For you remember, brethren, our labor and toil; for laboring night and day, that we might not be a burden to any of you, we preached to you the gospel of God.*

10 *You are witnesses, and God also, how devoutly and justly and blamelessly we behaved ourselves among you who believe;*

11 *as you know how we exhorted, and comforted, and [c]charged every one of you, as a father does his own children,*

12 *that you would walk worthy of God who calls you into His own kingdom and glory.*

Acts 20 :17-24

17 *From Miletus he sent to Ephesus and called for the elders of the church.*

18 *And when they had come to him, he said to them: "You know, from the first day that I came to Asia, in what manner I always lived among you,*

19 *serving the Lord with all humility, with many tears and trials which happened to me by the plotting of the Jews.*

20 *how I kept back nothing that was helpful, but proclaimed it to you, and taught you publicly and from house to house,*

21 *testifying to Jews, and also to Greeks, repentance toward God and faith toward our Lord Jesus Christ.*

22 *And see, now I go bound in the spirit to Jerusalem, not knowing the things that will happen to me there,*

23 *except that the Holy Spirit testifies in every city, saying that chains and tribulations await me.*

24 *[c]But none of these things move me; nor do I count my life dear to myself, so that I may finish my [d]race with joy, and the ministry which I received from the Lord Jesus, to testify to the gospel of the grace of God.*

Exercise 35

Can you provide examples of those in the Bible who demonstrated unethical behaviours and 3 things of what unethical behaviours not to have.

King Saul (1 Samuel 13–15)

- Unethical behavior: Disobedience, pride, jealousy.
- Example: Disobeyed God's command to completely destroy the Amalekites and their possessions; later became jealous of David and tried to kill him.

David (2 Samuel 11)

- Unethical behavior: Adultery, deception, murder.
- Example: Slept with Bathsheba, another man's wife, and then arranged for her husband, Uriah, to be killed in battle to cover it up.

Ananias and Sapphira (Acts 5:1–11)

- Unethical behavior: Lying, hypocrisy.
- Example: Lied about the amount of money they donated to the church to appear more generous than they really were. They were both struck dead.

Judas Iscariot (Matthew 26–27)

- Unethical behavior: Betrayal, greed.
- Example: Betrayed Jesus to the religious leaders for 30 pieces of silver,

leading to Jesus' arrest and crucifixion.

Achan (Joshua 7)

- Unethical behavior: Stealing, disobedience.
- Example: Took forbidden plunder from Jericho, causing Israel to lose a battle and bringing judgment on himself and his family.

The Religious Leaders (Various passages in the Gospels)

- Unethical behavior: Hypocrisy, legalism, injustice.
- Example: Jesus rebuked the Pharisees and scribes for pretending to be righteous while neglecting mercy, justice, and faithfulness (Matthew 23).

Ministerial Ethics in the church

Ministerial ethics in the church refers to the moral principles and professional standards that guide the conduct, responsibilities, and relationships of ministers and church leaders. Conducting ministerial ethics well is essential for maintaining integrity, trust, and effective spiritual leadership within the body of Christ.

Exercise 36 – Case Study – Group Session

In group session, make a detailed analysis of the following Case Study and advise Pastor James on ministerial ethics. Show him where he departed from his ministerial ethics and what steps he should now take.

Pastor James has been the pastor of the church in town for more than 10 years now. Based on the evangelist work he had done, the church had emerged. There was now a membership of thirty people. Most were town folks and worked in simple jobs. At least five of them, however, were professionally qualified and held jobs that afforded them a well-to-do lifestyle.

In the last three years or so, certain behaviours and conducts seemed to have crept into the church. For example, Pastor James began to appoint to the church Board those who were professional and who would more than likely gave more financially to the church. 1 Timothy 3:1–13; Titus 1:5–9; 1 Peter 5:1–4 no longer applied.

Some of the members began also to notice that Pastor James was beginning to be different in the way he conducted himself. One can only see him by appointment. Whatever he said could not be challenged. In fact, Pastor James would preach almost every Sunday to the members on sin and repentance, but how he lived and conducted himself did not line up with his messages. He was noted to have shouted and denigrated many members. Even the members of his own family were subject to his abuses. The Testimony and the witness of the church in the town and community were at stake.

Pastor James seemed to lay aside the financial integrity that was required of him. He made himself not only the sole signatory to the cheque account of the church, but he spent the funds of the church without caring to give an account for the same. He paid little or no attention to the principle found in 2 Corinthians 8:21.

Some mothers in the church were also having concerns about having one and one meetings with him or their daughters doing so. In fact, Sister Mary alleged that one day when he was counseling her, he appeared to be unable to maintain appropriate physical, emotional, and spiritual boundaries. She also complained that he tried to manipulate her and abused her spiritually.

Pastor James had also developed the habit of using the pulpit to say what others had told him in confidence and privacy. He did not care whether he had a legal/moral obligation to do so. There was a quarrel and conflict between Sister Brown and Sister Shirley. Pastor James however did not address issue biblically (Matthew 18:15–17). Clearly, he did not seek to promote reconciliation and peace within the congregation. He used the pulpit to resolve the matter. He was punitive. He showed no compassion and justice when dealing with the matter.

Pastor James took pleasure in divisiveness, gossip, or undermining fellow ministers. In fact, it was clear that he had no respect for Authority and Peers.

Obviously, therefore, Pastor James had descended. He was no longer faithful in Preaching and Teaching and handling the Word of God rightly (2 Timothy 2:15). A careful listening to his preaching and teaching would have shown that there was heresy and teaching for his personal gain. Several times he misquoted scriptures and gave interpretations that were not in sync with context. It was also observed that he had difficulties in locating reference texts and even books of the Bible.

Pastor James also removed and/or set aside all the safeguards and/or guardrails that would have kept him in check. There was no longer any written Ethics Policy or a ministerial code of ethics. There was no training on the subject matter. No one, including the members of the Board held him to account. Pastor James had no trusted mentor or peer groups from whom he could seek spiritual direction and fellowship.

Misconduct of Ministerial ethics and Restoration

Ministerial ethics are more than rules and regulations. They are a witness and a testimony to the transforming power of Christ. Hence, a morally upright and ethically sound minister leads not only by words but by example. He/she models a life that honors God and builds up His Church.

Yet over many years and it appears even more so today, there have been many pastors and church leaders who depart from their ministerial. The reasons are many and even interconnected. But their behaviours were so unethical and immoral that the world was shocked when their crimes and scandals became public.

Table 9 provides a list of some of those reasons:

Table 9

Reasons
Power and Pride: Unchecked pride, ego inflation, or a sense of entitlement can cause leaders to justify unethical behavior
Lack of Accountability: Absence of oversight and quardrails can may it possible for leaders to act without consequences or correction.
Moral or Spiritual Drift: Without continual personal spiritual discipline and reflection, leaders can slowly drift away from their ethical and spiritual foundations.
Temptation and Compromise: Leaders who yield to temptations especially financial, sexual open the doors to ethical failures
Burnout and Isolation: Leaders who do not manage stress well or who become isolated may make poor decisions out of desperation or fatigue.
Cultural or Institutional Pressures: Sometimes, the expectations or demands of the congregation or denomination may pressure leaders to cut ethical corners to appear successful.
Poor Mentoring or Training: A lack of proper ethical formation or mentoring can leave leaders unequipped to face the real-world challenges of ministry.

Exercise 37

From the list below, prioritize the top five reported areas or categories where ministers depart from ministerial ethics.:

1. Dishonesty and Deception
2. Abuse of Power and Control
3. Neglect of Personal and Spiritual Integrity
4. Financial Mismanagement or Greed
5. Sexual Misconduct

Sexual Misconduct is certainly the most prevalent and damaging. They include and are not limited to the following:

- premarital sex, adultery, and gay marriage
- Gay sex scandal

- Raping and drugging women
- Sexual abuse and fraud
- Sexual molestation and assault, including underage girls.
- sexual harassment, inappropriate touching
- multiple affairs
- child pornography
- cheating on their wives
- Prostitution
- pedophilia
- Homosexuality

Case 1

Many years ago, there was a noted televangelist who was scheduled to come to minister in Trinidad and Tobago, the land of my birth. Before his arrival the news broke that he was seen visiting the houses of prostitutes and perhaps engaging therein. The planners in Trinidad and Tobago were thrown into a quandary. Eventually they decided to withdraw the invitation. What was said of the televangelist was true. He was disbarred from ministering in the church. But years after he was found to be heading a thriving ministry carrying his own name.

Case 2

I recall another televangelist. He was perhaps one of the most sort after and widely known ministry in terms of presentation style, publication and audience reach. It was alleged that he misconducted himself because he was found associating with the "wrong" type of persons. That is those who were engaged in sexual exploitation. He fell in 2024. At the time of writing therefore, he has been completely taken off the TV and other media houses. He may not yet have been restored.

Case 3

He was one of the leading articulators and defender of faith. He successfully challenged university professors, atheists, people of other faiths and proven to be most convincing. After his death however it was reported that albeit married, he used to be engaged in many unacceptable sexual behaviours, including with young children. His organisation was disbanded, and his works are no longer seen or heard in the media.

Exercise 38

Using the text provided below, give in 200 words in each of 1 and 2, why the following specific reasons will cause church leaders to depart from ministerial ethics:

Table 10

Nos	Reasons	References
	Being unfaithful in marriage and dishonoring marriage vows	Genesis 2:24 Proverbs 5:19 Matthew 19:3-9 Colossians 3:19 Ephesians 5:25 1 Peter 3:7 Hebrews 13:4
	Not having or ceasing to have a daily time of personal prayer, Bible reading, and worship.	1 Thessalonians 5:15-17 Philippians 4:6-7

Addressing departure from Ministerial Ethics

Exercise 39

Question	Answer		
	Yes	No	Depends on
Should the minister who did not honour and/ or fail to function by ministerial ethics be restored?			

In my long years in church administration, I have found that most churches, especially those that are well structured and administered tend to do the following where there are breaches of ministerial ethics:

Diagram 41: Restoration Process

The outcome of the investigation and the types of disciplinary actions needed to be taken will proceed with the restoration process. For example, in these prior actions, the following may have to be done or be done.:

- Suspension of the church leader, pending the investigation
- He/she would have voluntarily confessed his/her misconduct—truthfully, specifically, and without excuses.
- A public acknowledgment may be necessary, depending on the visibility of the role and the nature of the offense.
- The disciplinary actions could include the church leader having to do a structured program that will include counseling and his/her ceasing all public ministries.
- Included will also be assisting the leader to renew his/her relationships especially with God, and his/her seeking reconciliation, especially with those who were hurt or harm

"He who conceals his sins does not prosper, but whoever confesses and renounces them finds mercy." — Proverbs 28:13

Now breaches involving criminal acts or persistent unrepentance are often not restorable. However, when restoration is appropriate, the process can be lengthy, but must balance truth, accountability, healing, and grace.

How then should those who have breached ministerial ethics be restored. Or should they be restored at all. Firstly, it is my view that Jesus would want them to be restored

Luke 22:31-34

31 *[d]And the Lord said, "Simon, Simon! Indeed, Satan has asked for you, that he may*
sift you as wheat.

32 *But I have prayed for you, that your faith should not fail; and when you have returned*
to Me, strengthen your brethren."

33 *But he said to Him, "Lord, I am ready to go with You, both to prison and to 0eath."*

34 *Then He said, "I tell you, Peter, the rooster shall not crow this day before you will*
deny three times that you know Me."

Secondly, restoration must include the following:

Diagram 42

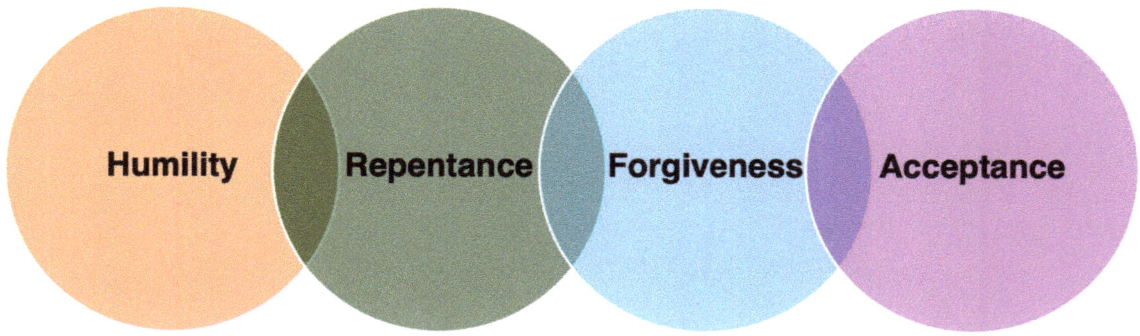

Humility

The church leader who had breached ministerial ethics and who now truly seeks reconciliation, and restoration must humble himself or herself

In the Bible, humility is a central and deeply valued virtue. It is often described as a posture of dependence on God, modesty about oneself, and a willingness to serve others rather than exalt oneself.

Table 11: Examples of humble people in the Bible

Names	Example	References
Moses	His hesitancy to accept leadership and constantly relied on God for guidance. His interceding tor the people	"Now Moses was very humble—more than any man on the face of the earth." *Numbers 12:3*
King David	His dependence on God. Repentant after his sinning with Bathsheba,	*Have mercy on me, O God... a broken and contrite heart you, God, will not despise." — Psalm 51:1,17*
Mary, the mother of Jesus	Humble obedience to God	*He has looked on the humble estate of his servant." — Luke 1:48*

Names	Example	References
Jesus Christ	washed His disciples' feet, served the poor, and willingly died on the cross for humanity.	*"Though he was in the form of God, [he] did not count equality with God a thing to be grasped..." — Philippians 2:6–8*
Apostle Paul	"the least of the apostles" and gave all credit to God's grace.	*"By the grace of God I am what I am." — 1 Corinthians 15:10*
King Nebuchadnezzar	"Is not this great Babylon, that I have built for a royal dwelling by my mighty power and for the honor of my majesty?"	Daniel 4:28-37

In the process, humility must also come to the community or people that the church leader had wronged. The truth is that when we see a person and in particular a leader falls, each of us should recognize our own individual sinful tendencies and the possibility of each of our own failure.

I recall well in my growing up in church that the Pastor would say that many would listen to the testimonies of others not so much as to help them in their weaknesses but rather to rejoice at what they heard them say. We must always remember that we too are exposed to yielding to temptations and sin. And with humility say "*There—but for the grace of God—go I.*"

Repentance

The church leader who had breached ministerial ethics and who now truly seeks reconciliation, and restoration must demonstrate true repentance.

The word *repentance* in the Bible literally means "the act of changing one's mind." True biblical repentance goes beyond remorse, regret, or feeling bad about one's sin. It involves more than merely turning away from sin. *Eerdmans Bible Dictionary* includes this definition of *repentance*: "In its fullest sense it is a term for a complete change of orientation involving a judgment upon the past and a deliberate redirection for the future."

Repentance in the Bible involves a complete change of heart and mind, leading to different actions (Acts 26:20). Repentance recognizes that our sin is offensive to God.

To repent is to make an about-face, a heart-directed turn away from self to God. Repentance sets us on a new trajectory, away from the past toward a future ruled by God's commands. Repentance acknowledges that the Lord reigns supreme over our existence. References:

"Repent therefore, and turn back, that your sins may be blotted out." – **Acts 3:19**

Return to the Lord your God, for he is gracious and merciful." – **Joel 2:13**

"Let the wicked forsake his way, and the unrighteous man his thoughts." – **Isaiah 55:7**

Bear fruit in keeping with repentance." – **Matthew 3:8**

Diagram 43: Key Aspects of Biblical Repentance:

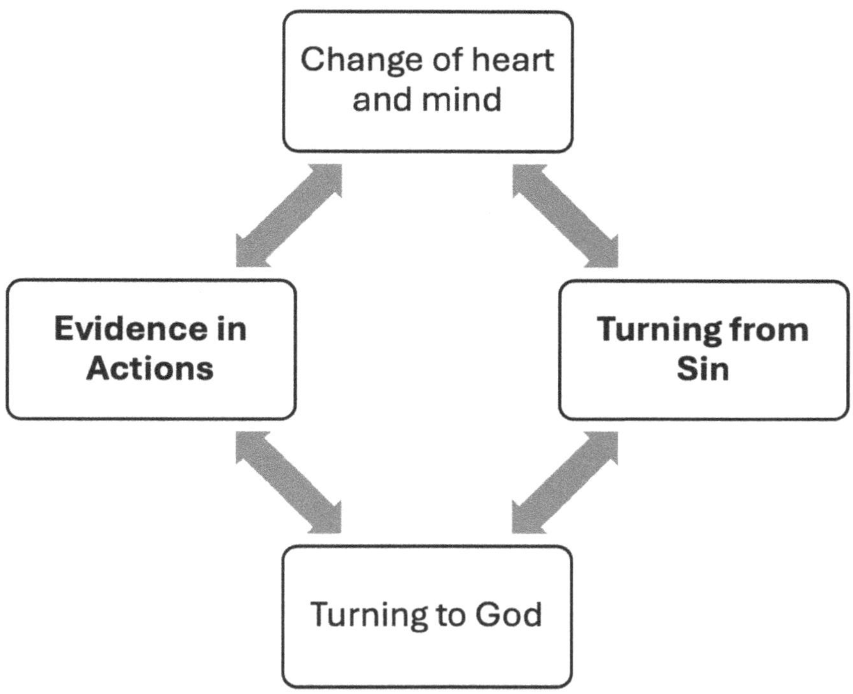

Forgiveness

Have those whom the church leader hurt or harmed when he breached ministerial ethics really have forgiven him/her?

Attempts have been made by others to explain forgiveness:

Desmond Tutu

Forgiveness says you are given another chance to make a new beginning."

Bryant H. McGill

"There is no love without forgiveness, and there is no forgiveness without love."

Martin Luther King Jr.

"Forgiveness is not an occasional act, it is a constant attitude." -

Jonathan Lockwood Huie

"Forgive others, not because they deserve forgiveness, but because you deserve peace."

Mahatma Gandhi

"The weak can never forgive. Forgiveness is the attribute of the strong."

Nelson Mandela is widely remembered for his remarkable stance on forgiveness and reconciliation after the end of apartheid in South Africa. Rather than seeking revenge against those who had oppressed and harmed black South Africans, he promoted unity and healing. Two of his most powerful statements were:

"As I walked out the door toward the gate that would lead to my freedom, I knew if I didn't leave my bitterness and hatred behind, I'd still be in prison."

"Courageous people do not fear forgiving, for the sake of peace."

More importantly however, is **Biblical Forgiveness. This** is the act of graciously releasing someone from the guilt and penalty of their offense, just as God forgives us through Jesus Christ. It is rooted in mercy, offered in love, and commanded for all who follow Christ.

Table 12: Key Aspects of Biblical Forgiveness

Aspects	References
Recognizing the wrong	*Luke 17:3 – "If your brother sins, rebuke him, and if he repents, forgive him."*
Releasing the offender	*Matthew 18:27* – The king "forgave the debt" and let the servant go.
Showing mercy and grace	*Ephesians 4:32 – "Be kind to one another... forgiving one another, as God in Christ forgave you."*
Making a decision (not based on feelings)	It is a **choice to obey God** and reflect His character (Colossians 3:13).
Refusing revenge or bitterness	*Romans 12:19 – "Beloved, never avenge yourselves..."* *Hebrews 12:15* warns against letting a "root of bitterness" grow

Pursuing peace and reconciliation	*2 Corinthians 5:18* – God has given us the "ministry of reconciliation."
Imitating Christ	*Luke 23:34 – "Father, forgive them, for they know not what they do."*

Forgiveness in the Bible [Compiled by The BibleStudyTools Staff]

The Bible emphasizes forgiveness as a fundamental aspect of Christian faith. In both the Old and New Testaments, God is portrayed as merciful and forgiving, encouraging believers to seek forgiveness and extend it to others. In the New Testament, Jesus Christ teaches the importance of forgiving others, as seen in the Lord's Prayer, where believers ask for forgiveness as they forgive those who trespass against them. The parable of the Unforgiving Servant further underscores the reciprocal nature of forgiveness, highlighting the expectation for believers to show mercy to others just as they have received mercy from God. Forgiveness is central to the biblical message, promoting reconciliation, compassion, and the transformative power of God's grace.

Hence it is this Biblical forgiveness of which and by which those who have been hurt and harmed must forgive the church leader who by his/her misconduct violated ministerial ethics

The following verses also clarify that forgiveness

Ephesians 4:32

Be kind to one another, tenderhearted, forgiving one another, as God in Christ forgave you.

Mark 11:25

And whenever you stand praying, forgive, if you have anything against anyone, so that your Father also who is in heaven may forgive you your trespasses."

1 John 1:9

If we confess our sins, he is faithful and just to forgive us our sins and to cleanse us from all unrighteousness.

Matthew 18:21-22

Then Peter came up and said to him, "Lord, how often will my brother sin against me, and I forgive him? As many as seven times?" Jesus said to him, "I do not say to you seven times, but seventy-seven times.

Matthew 6:14-15

For if you forgive others their trespasses, your heavenly Father will also forgive you, but if you do not forgive others their trespasses, neither will your Father forgive your trespasses.

Luke 6:37

"Judge not, and you will not be judged; condemn not, and you will not be condemned; forgive, and you will be forgiven;

Colossians 3:13

Bearing with one another and, if one has a complaint against another, forgiving each other; as the Lord has forgiven you, so you also must forgive.

Matthew 6:12

And forgive us our debts, as we also have forgiven our debtors.

Acts 2:38

And Peter said to them, "Repent and be baptized every one of you in the name of Jesus Christ for the forgiveness of your sins, and you will receive the gift of the Holy Spirit.

Ephesians 1:7

In him we have redemption through his blood, the forgiveness of our trespasses, according to the riches of his grace,

Acceptance

Many years ago, in the church that I attended in my homeland, Trinidad and Tobago, the Pastor cheated on his wife. He had an extra marital affair with a sister in the church. He left the church and went to the USA where he began another ministry. Some years later, he returned to Trinidad and Tobago. His wife refused to accept him, however. She was too hurt, and the pastor himself had never repented for his ministerial ethical misconduct.

Accepting someone back as if he/she has never hurt or harmed you is never easy. It takes the love and grace of God. In instance then of the minister who had misconducted himself or herself, it is not just the hurt or harmed person to do the acceptance. The church is also expected to accept him or her. Even the community is expected to do an acceptance.

Of such acceptance, to all the Bible provides much guidance however, especially when consideration is given to

Diagram 44

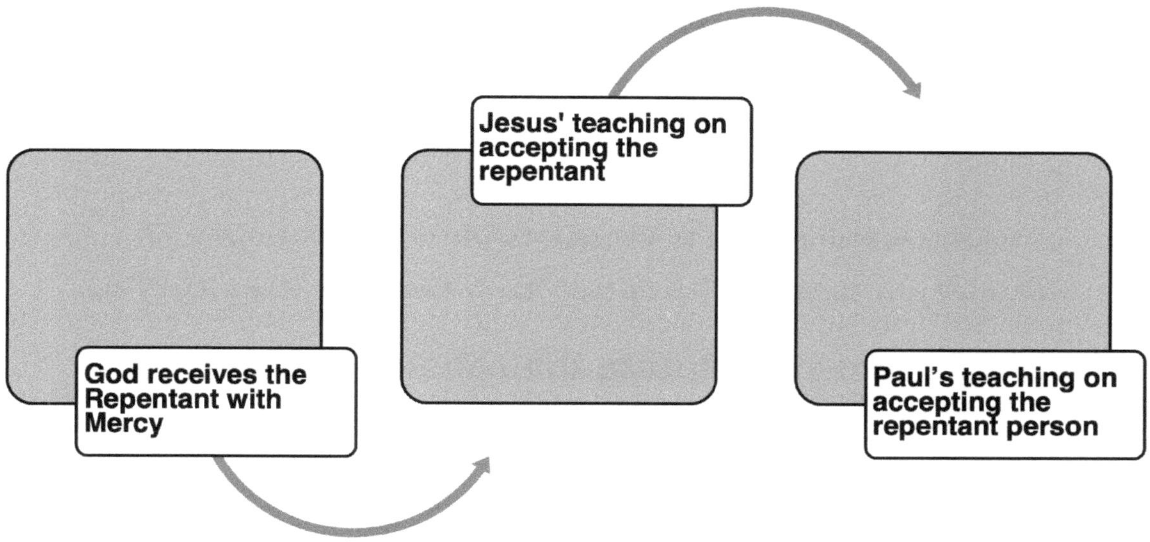

Diagram 45

God Receives the Repentant with Mercy	Isaiah 55:7 – *"Let the wicked forsake his way... let him return to the Lord, that He may have compassion on him... for He will abundantly pardon."* Psalm 51:17 – *"A broken and contrite heart, O God, you will not despise."* Luke 15:20 – *"While he was still a long way off, his father saw him and felt compassion... and ran and embraced him and kissed him."*

Jesus's teaching on accepting the repentant person

Forgiving freely and repeatedly (Luke 17:3-4)

"If your brother sins, rebuke him, and if he repents, forgive him. And if he sins against you seven times in the day and turns to you seven times, saying, 'I repent,' you must forgive him."

Welcoming joyfully and without shame (Luke 15)

The Parable of the Prodigal Son (Luke 15:11–32) -God's heart towards the repentant

There will be more joy in heaven over one sinner who repents than over ninety-nine righteous persons who need no repentance." – Luke 15:7

Restoring with compassion, not judgment (Luke 7)

A sinful woman anoints Jesus' feet in repentance, and Jesus forgives her publicly (Luke 7:36–50)

Valuing even the worst or the last-minute repentance (Luke 23)

"Truly I tell you, today you will be with me in Paradise." (Luke 23:39–43)

Paul's teaching on accepting the repentant person

a) Restore the repentant gently

Galatians 6:1 – *"Brothers, if anyone is caught in any transgression, you who are spiritual should restore him in a spirit of gentleness."*

Restoration is to be done gently and humbly.

b) Forgive and comfort them so they are not discouraged

2 Corinthians 2:7- so that, on the contrary, you *ought* rather to forgive and comfort *him*, lest perhaps such a one be swallowed up with too much sorrow.

c) Reaffirm our love and accept them back into the community (2 Corinthians 2:8)

2 Corinthians 2:8 Therefore I urge you to reaffirm *your* love to him.

d) Remember **our own pasts** and God's grace to us all (1 Corinthians 6:11)

1 Corinthians 6:11 -And such were some of you. But you were washed, but you were [a]sanctified, but you were justified in the name of the Lord Jesus and by the Spirit of our God.

Conclusively then, the acceptance process or welcoming back the repentant will include and not be limited to

Diagram 46

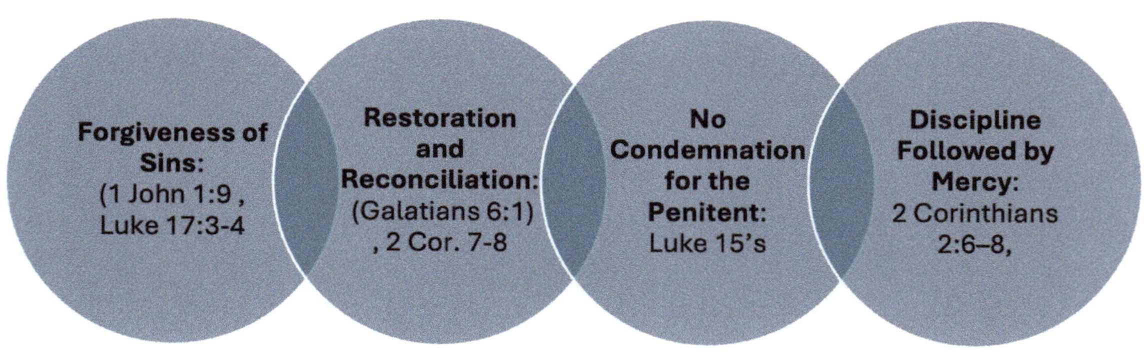

Finally, Churches and individual Christians often struggle with working through the restoration of a leader. A writer on the subject submitted:

> *"Sins of an egregious nature—and the dimensions of that are subjective—compromise a pastor's effectiveness and make it obvious that a man is not qualified or even able to shepherd for the time being, even if he repents," .*
>
> *Restoration is going to involve others. A pastor should not assume this can be done individually. "A pastor who has sinned cannot restore himself nor declare himself restored," .*
>
> *Other churches and pastors should be involved in the process. "Church leaders should enlist another congregation and pastor to receive and shepherd the fallen pastor through the long, hard road of repentance."*
>
> *As others walk with the fallen leader, they "need to watch for signs of brokenness, repentance, attempts at restoration and reconciliation, humility, and a fresh desire for Christ—not merely ministry."*
>
> *A further writer says restoration to the pastoral leadership role is "not usually the best course of action" for the church or the leader.*
>
> *"Restored leaders can continue to make significant contributions to kingdom advancement and disciple-making, but they don't have to do it a formal pastoral role," .*
>
> *"The consequences of sin sometimes cause us to forfeit certain privileges, but they don't negate our value in the fellowship and mission of Christ's church."*

Exercise 40

A Pastor was found to have lied to the members of the church concerning his past life and has been dishonest in his ways towards them.

Advise that Pastor what he/she should do?

Exercise 41

Are the following ethical behaviours

Nos	Actions	Yes	No
1	The Pastor takes a cheque signed by his wife and himself.		
2	Officers and leaders of the church are elected by voting		
3	No business meetings are held with the members		
4	Disciplinary actions are not taken on a member because he/she pays large sums in tithes and gives generously.		
5	The Pastor and leaders attend to ministry of the word and prayer ONLY and not to administrative matters		
6	Incomplete records are kept of the finances of the church		
7	The Pastor has compromised his position but refuses to resign		

Ministerial Code of Ethics [Downloaded ChatGPT]

A ministerial code of ethics is a set of principles and guidelines that govern the behavior, responsibilities, and conduct of individuals serving in ministerial or pastoral roles within religious organizations. These codes aim to ensure that ministers act with integrity, accountability, and respect in both their personal and professional lives.

Key Elements of a Ministerial Code of Ethics

1. *Spiritual and Personal Integrity*
   - *Live a life consistent with the teachings of the faith.*
   - *Practice regular prayer, study, and spiritual growth.*
   - *Be honest, humble, and trustworthy in all dealings.*
2. *Professional Conduct*
   - *Maintain appropriate boundaries in pastoral relationships.*
   - *Avoid conflicts of interest, favoritism, or abuse of power.*
   - *Handle church finances, counseling, and administrative duties with transparency.*
3. *Confidentiality*
   - *Respect the privacy of individuals and uphold confidentiality, especially in counseling situations, unless there is a risk of harm.*

4. *Respect for Others*
    - *Treat all individuals with dignity and fairness, regardless of background.*
    - *Promote peace, justice, and reconciliation in the community.*
5. *Accountability*
    - *Submit to appropriate oversight by denominational or church authorities.*
    - *Be open to correction and committed to growth and ethical responsibility.*
6. *Sexual Ethics*
    - *Remain faithful in marriage and celibate in singleness.*
    - *Avoid any form of sexual misconduct or exploitation.*
7. *Legal and Ethical Compliance*
    - *Obey civil laws unless they directly contradict religious convictions.*
    - *Report illegal or unethical behavior appropriately.*

Purpose of a Ministerial Code of Ethics

- *Protects the integrity of the ministry and the reputation of the church.*
- *Guides ministers in making difficult moral or pastoral decisions.*
- *Supports accountability and trust within the faith community.*
- *Prevents misconduct and promotes healthy relationships and environments.*

Example of Ministerial Code of Ethics

I had been a Bishop with the New Testament Church of God in England and Wales and served as Pastor, of the church located in Romford for fifteen years. The following then

1. **Theologically Sound Leadership**

    NTCG emphasizes equipping ministers and lay leaders to manage churches effectively. This includes ongoing theological and practical leadership training, ensuring that leaders are well-prepared to serve their congregations.

2. **Community Engagement and Justice**

    The church is committed to living out its convictions through actions and advocacy. This involves loving neighbors, doing justice, loving mercy, and advocating for the rights of destitute, reflecting a deep commitment to social justice.

3. **Equality and Inclusion**

   NTCG upholds values such as equality of men and women, full access for all abilities, and the safe nurturing of children and young people. These values ensure that ministers foster inclusive and respectful environments.

4. **Spiritual Discipline and Holiness**

   As a Pentecostal denomination, NTCG encourages spiritual discipline like prayer and fasting. Ministers are expected to lead by example in these areas, promoting spiritual growth within their communities.

5. **Ministerial Development and Accountability**

   The church commits to identifying and developing individuals with leadership gifts, challenging them to become servant-leaders. This includes providing relevant resources and training opportunities for both clergy and laity.

Summary

Among others, Ethics can be defined as

> *a system of moral principles. They affect how people make decisions and lead their lives. Ethics is concerned with what is good for individuals and society and is also described as moral philosophy.*
>
> *is the study of right and wrong behavior. It deals with the principles that guide how people should act toward others, themselves, and society as a whole. Ethics helps us make decisions that align with values like honesty, fairness, respect, and responsibility.*

Simple understanding and/or definition of Ethics, Christian ethics, church ethics, and ministerial ethics include

Ethics is about doing the right thing, especially when facing difficult decisions

Church ethics is about practicing what is preached

Christian ethics seeks to answer the question: "How should a follower of Christ live?"

Ministerial ethics is about character, conduct, and calling—how a minister represents Christ faithfully in public and private life.

Key aspects Ethics, Christian ethics, church ethics, and ministerial ethics can be summarized as follows:

Table 13

Ethics	**Christian Ethics**	**Church Ethics**	**Ministerial Ethics**
about doing the right thing, especially when facing difficult decisions	answer the question: "How should a follower of Christ live? • Love (Agape) • Imitation Christ • The Ten Commandments	about practicing what is preached reflecting the character of Christ and the teachings of the Bible.	about character, conduct, and calling—how a minister represents Christ faithfully in public and private life
Moral Principles e.g. *honesty, justice, kindness* : Right vs. Wrong: *based on reason, conscience, laws, or cultural values* Sources of Ethics: - *Philosophy, religion, culture, norms*	• The Beatitudes • The Fruit of the Spirit • Justice and Mercy • Sanctity of Life • Stewardship • Community and Forgiveness	• Moral Behavior in the Church Community: -, • Ethical Leadership: • Justice, Fairness: • Conflict Resolution: • addressing disagreements • witness to the world	• Personal Integrity • Confidentiality • Accountability • Avoiding Abuse of Power • Relationships • Financial Integrity: • Doctrinal Honesty: • Respect for Other Ministries

The focus was given to Ministerial Ethics. In that context therefore, examination and explanation were given to

1. Ethics – The perspective of leading Pastors
2. Ethical Behaviour -Biblical example
3. Ministerial Ethics in the church
4. Misconduct of Ministerial ethics and Restoration
5. Ministerial Code of Ethics

www.ingramcontent.com/pod-product-compliance
Lightning Source LLC
LaVergne TN
LVHW071218210926
848482LV00015B/839